FRÉDÉRIC MORVAN

Objective
Louvre

THE GUIDE
TO FAMILY VISITS

Translation by Jonathan Sly

ACTES SUD JUNIOR   LOUVRE   MUSÉE DU LOUVRE ÉDITIONS

Contents

NOTICE
- Visitors are advised to pick up the free floorplan from the Reception
(see also floorplan at the end of this guidebook)
- The room numbers indicated correspond to those of the department to which
the works belong;
- Certain artworks may be temporarily absent due to research, restoration,
loans to exhibitions, or gallery refurbishment work;
- The Louvre's collection of masterpieces of Islamic art will feature in a later
publication, after the refurbishment of the relative department has been completed.

In the footsteps of history...

This guidebook is designed to help young people (and the adults accompanying them!) to explore and discover the treasures of the largest museum in the entire world.

The guide takes visitors on a historical journey from east to west, starting with the birth of writing in Mesopotamia and leading to the French Revolution.

Each tour is fully complemented with illustrations to help visitors identify the various phases of cultural development, which are clearly explained and feature the cultural milestones for each period.

The guide is devised to be stimulating for adults as well, and there are special activities for younger children to encourage them to explore.

It is not our ambition to turn our visitors into experts in art history, but to accompany you through the labyrinth of the Louvre, prompting ideas and providing clues to allow you to decide entirely for yourselves which route to take and what to see.

Although each tour is calculated to take around two hours, you are free to extend your visit and discover other rooms and works as well; you might even like to explore the museum's vast library.

After you have got an idea of the collections, you can find out more about the museum building itself on the website (www.louvre.fr), where there is also a virtual tour of the halls, plus further details of the Louvre's activities for both adults and children, such as learning workshops, guided tours, and so forth.

Please note that although the museum itself is closed on Tuesdays, the palace and Tuileries Gardens remain open to the public, and of course it is worth visiting the entire area around the museum, which is one of the oldest in Paris.

So, get your pen and paper ready: the museum is all yours!

The Louvre is the largest museum in the world. Like some vast, walk-through history-book, it offers a living testament of every imaginable form of artistic expression produced by humankind, from the earliest civilisations right up to the 19th century. It is fairly easy to lose one's bearings in this maze of history, but from your first visit you will begin to get an idea of the vast number of works on display, which include some of the absolute masterpieces of human creativity. So, where better to start than with a selection of the Louvre's most prized possessions: the sublime *Venus de Milo*, David's *Consecration of Emperor Napoleon*, the imposing *Winged Victory of Samothrace*, and perhaps the museum's best-known work, the supremely enigmatic *Mona Lisa*.

EIGHT CENTURIES OF HISTORY:
FROM PALACE TO MUSEUM
The foundations of the medieval Louvre

In addition to the treasures inside the Louvre, the walls containing them are also worth exploring. The building itself was once a fortified castle, built around 1200 by King Philippe II Augustus to protect Paris. Today, the base of the walls and towers of the castle are still visible. During its eight centuries of history, the building was expanded and transformed. Under François I (1494-1547), the castle was reworked as an elegant Renaissance-style palatial home; Louis XIV (1638-1715) however abandoned its vastness for Versailles; in the 19th century it was once more occupied by kings and emperors. The site is a cornerstone of French history, and offers a compendium of the development of French architecture through the centuries.

A Tour of the Principal Masterpieces

▶▶ *Follow the east wall up to the Great Sphinx of Tanis in pink granite (see p. 29), which commands the entrance to the Egyptian Antiquities department. Then take the left staircase to the ground floor, and walk through all the rooms to reach the grand staircase leading to the first floor and the gallery of Egyptian masterpieces. Head to Room 22, which is home to the most famous scribe of Antiquity.*

Living for eternity

This painted limestone statue, with its inlaid quartz and copper eyes, was made around 2500 BC. Apart from its age, the statue is also remarkable for the vivacity of its facial expression.

▲ *The Seated Scribe*, ca. 2600-2350 BC.
Painted limestone statue, quartz eyes set in copper. H. 53.7 cm, W. 44 cm.

Why did the Egyptians put such statues in their tombs?

The ancient Egyptians' major preoccupation during life was to achieve immortality. This is why they had their corpses mummified before entombment, so as to preserve their appearance in the afterlife, and they were buried together with realistic pictures and statues of themselves to ensure their "survival" after death. This scribe statue was made around the same time as the Great Pyramids; if you look at it for long enough, it seems to come to life.

▶▶ *As you walk back the way you came, stop in Room 25 before the huge statue of the pharaoh Amenophis IV, better known as Akhenaton, who reigned in the 14th century BC.*

The mystical pharaoh

Like all the statues of this period, the pharaoh's face is strangely elongated. In more ways than one, Akhenaton stands out from the long series of Egyptian pharaohs.

Why is Akhenaton so special?

Alongside Ramses II and Cleopatra, Akhenaton was probably one of the most famous figures of pharaonic Egypt, as famous as his wife Nefertiti. Akhenaton ruled at the height of Egyptian society in the 8th dynasty, and revolutionised the country's religion by giving primacy to a single deity, the sun-god Aton. He also founded a new capital, Amarna. Meanwhile, the artists of this period also radically transformed the way they portrayed the human form, making their figures androgynous and more refined.

How was the statue discovered?

Like many of the Louvre's antiquities, the statue was a gift, in this case from the Egyptian government, in gratitude for France's help in saving the Nubian monuments threatened by the construction of the Aswan Dam.

▶ *King Amenophis IV, or Akhenaton, ca. 1350 BC. Sandstone. H. 1.37 m.*

▶▶ *Now leave the Egyptian Antiquities department and cross to the end of the Greek Antiquities department until you reach the room devoted to English painting, where a statue of one of the most important goddesses of Greek civilisation has been provisionally installed. (Note: this work is liable to change room.)*

The archetype of absolute beauty

The epitome of female grace, this statue is one of the most important of all the Hellenistic Greek sculptures that have reached us, and was carved a hundred years before the birth of Christ. Because she represents the Greek goddess of love (Aphrodite), her breasts are bare, while a swirl of drapery bestows modesty and adds dynamism to the gentle twist of her body.

Where does the statue come from?

The statue was discovered in 1820 on the island of Milo, in the archipelago of the Cyclades. Several questions regarding the statue remain because her arms have never been found, and therefore the symbols she must have been carrying are a mystery. The name of the sculptor is also unknown. When King Louis XVIII purchased it for the Louvre, he initially wanted to add new arms, but then decided against this for fear of ruining the statue.

◀ *Aphrodite,* known as the *Venus de Milo,* ca. 130-100 BC. Marble. H. 2.02 m.

▶▶ *When you leave the* Venus de Milo, *head towards the Rotonde d'Apollon, which leads to the Apollo Gallery, where there are a number of remarkable treasures, including the diamonds, crowns, and precious stones forming the remains of the French crown jewels. The decor of the Royal Gallery, the work of Louis XIV's head painter Charles Le Brun, is one of the most beautiful in the palace and was the inspiration for the Hall of Mirrors at the Château of Versailles. As you leave on your left, you will find yourself on the landing of the vast Daru staircase.*

◄ *The Winged Victory of Samothrace,* ca. 190 BC.
Statue in Paros marble, vessel in grey Lartos
(Rhodes) marble (the right wing
is a plaster reconstruction).
H. 3.28 m.

Nike: The goddess of victory

The sense of movement in this work comes from the energy of the outspread wings, and spray-sodden draperies clinging to the figure's body. The Nike (Victory) figurehead, discovered in 1863 by a French diplomat, is magnificently set on the prow of a ship dominating the Daru staircase. The statue's hand, which was only found in 1950, is conserved in a glass case nearby.

What does this monument symbolise?

The statue was originally located overlooking the sea atop a cliff on the isle of Samothrace, in the Aegean Sea, and was probably a gift to the gods to ward off shipwrecks and bring success in battle. The statue commemorates a naval victory over Rhodes around 190 BC.

▶▶ *To the left of the* Winged Victory, *in the vestibule of the Napoleon I Museum, the department of Italian Painting begins. Italian painting was the passion of French kings from the Renaissance onwards, and was long considered the model of art in Europe. The vestibule opens onto the Salon Carré, leading to the Grand Gallery, which runs along the length of the Seine, and which originally led to the Tuileries Palace. The gallery is the most impressive in the museum, and measures nearly 450 metres long. Walk to the middle of the gallery and enter Room 6, marked with the name* La Joconde, *to your right. The work sits with the masterpieces of Venetian painting, in particular the famous* Wedding Feast at Cana *by Paolo Veronese (see p. 99).*

A world-famous smile

A beautiful woman seated in a loggia, her hands crossed, posing before the Tuscan landscape, painted in a blue-misted *sfumato* haze. Her face is lit up with an enigmatic smile, and her eyes seem to stare at us. The fine black muslin veil over her hair could mean that she is an allegory of maternity, but she is also considered to be the symbol of serenity (*jucunda* in Latin).

How did it reach the Louvre?

When King François I invited Leonardo da Vinci to live in France towards the end of his life, he fell in love with this painting and purchased it from the artist. His successors considered it the highlight of the royal collection, and Louis XIV hung it in his Versailles study, while Napoleon I hung it above his bed in the Tuileries.

Why is it so famous?

The portrait's mysterious smile and uncertain identity, along with the fascinating character of the artist, have led to many theories about the work's origins. Some even believe that it is a self-portrait, dressed as a woman. The painting was stolen in 1911 by an Italian glazier, but was found two years later.

▶ Leonardo di ser Piero da Vinci (1452-1519), *Portrait of Lisa Gherardini*, known as the *Mona Lisa*, 1503-06. Oil on wood. 77 x 53 cm.

▶▶ *At the back of the room, behind the* Mona Lisa, *the Salon Denon is another spectacular room. The Neoclassical painting of the late 18th century and early 19th was marked by Graeco-Roman inspiration. Turn right and proceed into the Salle Daru (Room 75).*

The Emperor's glory

Among the major works by the painter David conserved in the Louvre - *The Oath of the Horatii* (see p. 124), *The Intervention of the Sabine Women*, *Leonidas at Thermopylae*, *The Lictors Bring to Brutus the Bodies of his Sons* - most are of Antique inspiration. The *Consecration of Emperor Napoleon* however depicts a real event, although the painter allowed himself a certain amount of poetic license, and introduced a large number of people into the frame (191 in all), some of whom did not even attend the coronation.

▲ Jacques-Louis David (1748-1825), *The Consecration of Emperor Napoleon and the Coronation of Empress Josephine in the Cathedral of Notre-Dame*, Paris, 1806/07. Oil on canvas. 6.21 x 9.79 m.

Which moment did David choose?

David chose to depict the moment when Napoleon places the imperial crown on his wife's head. Napoleon is depicted as a Roman emperor, crowned with a golden laurel wreath. It is as if all present are holding their breath. Only the choirboys, on the far right, seem to be more engrossed in the sword of the handsome Eugène de Beauharnais.

Who is sitting behind Napoleon?

Pope Pius VII, whom Napoleon summoned specially from Rome, only to cast him as an extra. We can also see the whole Bonaparte family, as well as the major dignitaries of the regime. David depicted himself too, in a green scholar's outfit, in the process of drawing. See if you can find him.

13

▶▶ *Go back through the Salle Denon and head into the other large red room, the Salle Mollien (Room 77). Here you will witness the great talent of the French Romantic painters, in particular Géricault and Delacroix, and their works depicting topical contemporary events.*

▲ Théodore Géricault (1791-1824), *The Raft of the Medusa*, 1819. Oil on canvas. 4.91 x 7.16 m.

1819: Scandal at the Louvre

On a makeshift raft adrift in the ocean, the fifteen survivors of a crew of 150 glimpse a ship on the horizon. It was this moment that the painter chose to relate the harrowing story of a shipwreck of a French frigate, the *Medusa*, off the African coast in 1816. Its pyramidal composition has a Classical inspiration, while the brutal realism of the corpses is a manifesto of Romanticism.

Why did the painting cause such a stir when it was unveiled?
First, because it shows the full extent of the horror and degradation experienced by the victims of the shipwreck. And secondly, because it is loaded with political subtexts: the shipwreck was caused by the incompetence of its captain, giving rise to great controversy for the recently restored French monarchy. The presence of a black man on the raft was also interpreted as a protest against slavery, abolished after the Revolution but reinstated under Napoleon I.

"Les Trois Glorieuses"

The three-day Revolution in July 1830, known as "Les Trois Glorieuses", which brought an end to the Restoration monarchy, was depicted by Eugène Delacroix as a bare-breasted woman, armed with a rifle and brandishing the French flag. The image has since become the symbol of the French Republic. The spirited Liberty is shown leading the population over rubble and corpses in rebellion against Charles X. In the background we see the towers of Notre Dame cathedral, the heart of the city in revolt.

▲ Eugène Delacroix (1789-1863), *Liberty Guiding the People*, 1830. Oil on canvas. 2.60 x 3.25 m.

Who is the young boy to the right of Liberty?

The boy is Gavroche, the archetype of Parisian street urchins, hero of Victor Hugo's *Les Misérables*, and the neglected son of the Thénardiers. Gavroche dies on the barricades, and his famous death-song runs:

> *". . . Joy is my nature,*
> *Because of Voltaire,*
> *Misery is my trousseau,*
> *Because of Rousseau . . ."*

▶▶ *At the end of the Salle Mollien,
take the large staircase to the ground
floor and the Italian Sculpture room.
Here you will find two unfinished statues
by one of the greatest painters, sculptors,
architects, engineers, and poets of all time:
Michelangelo.*

▶ Michelangelo Buonarroti,
known as Michelangelo (1475-1564),
Slaves, also called *The Rebellious
Slave and the Dying Slave*.
1513-15. Marble. H. 2.09 m.

The soul enslaved

From behind, these two large
statues are merely roughed-out
and unfinished. From the front,
however, the sculptor's art has
produced figures as beautiful
as Classical sculptures. The rebel
slave writhes vigorously to rid
himself of his bonds;
his companion meanwhile
appears to be in the throes
of death.

Why are the sculptures unfinished?
They were originally intended for the
tomb of Pope Julius II in Rome, the same
pope who commissioned the artist's work
in the Sistine Chapel. But the tomb
project was abandoned, and Michelangelo
offered them unfinished to a friend as
a gift, who in turn donated them to
the king of France. They first appeared
in the Louvre during the Revolution.

What do the *Slaves* represent?
Their message is not a criticism of slavery, and the sculptures are rather a form
of mystical allegory inspired by Plato, whereby the human soul is imprisoned
within the body like a slave. They could therefore represent the opposition
between spirituality and sensuality, the divine world and terrestrial existence.
The rebel slave tries to extricate himself, whereas the naked, dying slave seems
to writhe in sensual abandon.

▶▶ *At the other end of the Michelangelo Gallery, you may like to take in another allegory that was inspired by Antiquity,* Eros and Psyche *by Antonio Canova. Next turn right into the Salle du Manège (Room A), and take the staircase leading to the Pyramid. Walk in the direction of the Richelieu wing where, on the ground floor, is the French Sculpture department.*
The former courtyards of the palace now have glazed roofs, and house several major works of French Classicism that formerly stood in public spaces or in royal homes.
Turn left into the Cour Marly, with its magnificent horse statues.

For his Majesty's pleasure

There are two groups of equine sculptures in this courtyard, produced by two sculptors, Antoine Coysevox and Guillaume Coustou, uncle and nephew, who produced *Mercury Riding Pegasus* and *Horses Restrained by Grooms*. The two statues successively decorated the horse pond at Louis XIV's favourite château at Marly near Paris. While Coysevox's horses appear tame, Coustou's convey surprising grace, energy and naturalism in their forms and movements.

▸ Guillaume Coustou (1677-1746), *Horse Restrained by a Groom*, known as the *Marly Horse*. 1739-45. Marble. H. 3.55 m.

Why did the statues leave Marly?
The château was destroyed. The Coysevox groups were installed at the entrance to the Tuileries in 1719, and the Coustou groups were placed at the bottom of the Champs-Elysées after the Revolution. The originals were recently relocated to the Louvre, and replaced with copies in Marly and in Paris.

Why are they considered to be masterpieces?
The statues were hewn from Carrara marble by the court's official artists, and they represent the pinnacle of Classicism in France, which since the reign of Louis XIV had become the model for art in Europe. The Louvre's Colonnade, the Château of Versailles, and other royal homes with their painted and sculpted decor are also emblematic of this era.

▶▶ *To reach the second floor, and the French paintings of the Northern Schools, take the large escalator created by the American architect Ieoh Ming Pei, commissioned by President François Mitterand, when the Louvre was restructured in 1983. A very large number of masterpieces are housed here; not only is it the most substantial collection of French painting in the world, but the best of Dutch and Flemish painting also figure highly, as French kings were particularly keen collectors.*
To reach the Dutch paintings, enter Room 19 (Flanders, 17th century); on the right there is the Medici Gallery containing Rubens's famous masterpiece relating the history of Henri IV and Marie de' Medici in 24 paintings (see p. 108). From here you may access Room 38.

Grandeur in simplicity

In a magical light and an atmosphere of contemplation, a girl pores over her lacework, a speciality of Flanders. Before her lies a Bible, bringing a moral and religious feel to the painting. The same silence, encapsulated in a light effect of similar magnificence, can be found in another of Vermeer's famous tableaux, *The Astronomer*, also in Room 38.

▲ Johannes Vermeer (1632-75), *The Lacemaker*, ca. 1665-70. Oil on canvas mounted on wood. 24 x 21 cm.

Why the passion for collecting these works?

Dutch and Flemish painters were masters in the art of painting scenes of private life. Their work is a far cry from the vast constructions of French historical painting. Their art is imbued with amazing realism and illusionism, and speaks volumes about its period.

▶▶ *Go back the way you came through the French painting rooms to reach Room 28, devoted to Georges de La Tour. On your way you can also admire, in the Rotonde (Room 16), the* Four Seasons *by one of France's most famous artists, Nicolas Poussin.*

A moral fable

A young elegantly dressed man is busy playing cards with two women and another man, the cheat of the title, who is concealing cards behind his back. The elegant young man is so engrossed in his hand that he seems not to notice something is afoot. The play of glances brings the scene to life and, humorous as it is, it also contains a moral message, warning youth against the dangers of gambling, women, and wine.

▲ Georges de La Tour (1593-1652), *The Cheat with the Ace of Diamonds,* ca. 1635. Oil on canvas. 1.07 x 1.46 m.

What does the fable mean?

The innocent young man has made himself vulnerable to the morally unacceptable temptations of the 17th century: gambling, alcohol, and lust. Not only does the young man risk losing the game - and his money - he is also liable to finish the evening drunk in the arms of a courtesan.

KIDS' CORNER
Look at the other paintings by this artist, inspired by the Italian painter Caravaggio. There are a few of them in the Grand Gallery. The light effects in the night scenes, with their candlelight and darkness, are remarkable.

Writing originated thousands of years ago. The origins of language date back some 200,000 years; mankind started to draw on cave walls 20,000 years ago. In 7000 or 6000 BC, the Chinese invented the first form of writing, which is still used today. Cuneiform writing appeared in Mesopotamia around 3300 BC. With the creation of the first towns, civil society was established. Writing became necessary for bookkeeping in agriculture and trade, as well as in writing laws.

A TALE IN SIGNS AND PICTURES
Victory Stele of Eannatum, known as the *Stele of Vultures,* **ca. 2450 BC**
A bearded giant stands by a net containing prisoners and beats them with a club. In his left hand, he is holding a divine emblem, an eagle with the head of a lion. The figure is probably that of Ningirsou, the guardian god of the town of Lagash, or that of its king, Eannatum. The text in the lower part of the stele explains the meaning of the scene depicted. The stele commemorates the victory of Lagash over the neighbouring town of Oumma, both situated in the land of Sumer. Both towns were city-states of Mesopotamia (today's Iraq), where civilisation first developed. This is one of the earliest "historical accounts" ever found.

The origins of writing
in Mesopotamia

The invention of writing

While our alphabet is made up of 26 abstract shapes called "letters", which are used to form words, ancient forms of writing are much more complex and feature a huge range of symbols. One of the early forms, cuneiform, with its wedge shaped symbols, was used by many languages - Sumerian, Akkadian, Assyrian, etc. - up to the 7th century BC. Cuneiform writing was invented for bookkeeping in agriculture, but it was also used to record the history of these civilisations, which has helped us understand them today.

An accountant's language

Accountancy records were kept on slate and stone tablets covered in signs, some of which are clearly figurative, such as ears of corn, gardens, fields, irrigation canals, animals, rising or setting suns, female genitalia, or bearded masculine heads. Numbers were represented by small holes.

▶ *Pre-cuneiform accountancy tablet (an archaic land sale contract),* ca. 3300-3200 BC, Case 3. W. 10.5 cm.

What do the signs mean?
The signs record the accounts relating to agricultural production, the storage of harvests, trade between states, and land and slave sales in the early Mesopotamian cities.

Why are some tablets in clay and others in stone?
For daily accountancy, wet clay was the most practical material; symbols could be impressed quickly using a reed. For more substantial texts, more durable materials were preferred, even if they took much longer to produce.

▶ Sumerian characters in the 4th millennium BC were originally pictographic, that is to say they represented objects or beings, using a picture or symbol. This figurative form of writing gradually evolved more abstract characters, created with a reed whittled to a point, which made nail-like imprints on wet clay (cuneus in Latin, hence the word "cuneiform").
The combination of these signs was used to transcribe the sounds of spoken language.

EXAMPLES OF THE EVOLUTION OF A WRITING SYSTEM

Man

Eat

Walk

God, Star

Ram

Historical archives

Here is an earthenware cone covered in miniscule signs that are sometimes almost impossible to read. Trained scribes were required to carry out such painstaking work for Sumerian towns.

What were the cones used for?
The cones are the oldest historical archives to be discovered in the remains of Sumerian cities. They were conserved to record the achievements of kings, but also as a justification of their territory and possessions.

▲ *Cone of Entemena, Prince of Lagash*, ca. 2400 BC. Earthenware. H. 27 cm.

What does the *Cone of Entemena* relate?
This particular cone tells the history of the turbulent relations between the states of Lagash and Oumma along their common border. It appears that it was Prince Entemena who put an end to land disputes by reinstating a "talus-frontier", also demanded by Ila, the Prince of Oumma. Another cone in the same case informs us that it was Oumma who finally won this particular battle.

KID'S CORNER
Take a look at the very animated figures of humans and animals in Cases 5 and 6 in the same room, like the *Relief of Ur-Nanshe, King of Lagash*.

Writings celebrating the glory of the prince, minister of men

There are a great many monuments and statues covered in cuneiform writing, which tell us a great deal about the life and work of the Mesopotamian princes. One such sovereign was Gudea, prince of Lagash, who built many temples in honour of the god Ningirsu. The image of him described in his writings is that of a devout and scholarly king.

A monument to writing

Here is a Diorite obelisk, a hard black stone, covered in cuneiform writing regularly arranged in 1519 compartments.

Where does this black stone come from?
From across the sea, on the other side of the Persian, Arabian and even, possibly the Egyptian Gulf. King Manishtusu had to make specially equipped ships to bring back this precious material to Akkad.

What language is it in?
The writing on the stone is not Sumerian but another language, Akkadian. The Akkadian language used the same cuneiform symbols as Sumerian, which meant that different people could communicate with each other using the shared system of signs.

▲ *Obelisk of Manishtusu, king of Akkad,* ca. 2270 BC. Diorite. 1.40 x 0.60 m.

What is written on the obelisk?
The obelisk tells the story of Akkad, a flourishing city in the north of Sumer. The writings also tell of land purchased by the king and offered to his officers to guarantee their loyalty, and consequently the political stability of his kingdom.

The devout Gudea, scholar, king, and builder

Among the many statues of Gudea, this one, depicting the sovereign carrying a vase overflowing with water and fish, is the most remarkable. The sovereign is wearing the royal headgear of a wool or fur hat, accompanied by a long smooth, possibly linen robe with fringes, which reveals one shoulder. Like most of the other statues of him, the cuneiform writing covers a large part of the robe and back, and even his bare shoulder.

Why the obsession with writing?
The writings tell of the sovereign's role as an intellectual, architect, and benefactor, and serve to immortalise his memory. On this statue is written "Gudea, prince of Lagash, who built the temple of Ningishzidda and the temple of Geshtinnana".

▶ *Gudea and Flowing Vase*, ca. 2120 BC. Dolerite. 62 x 25.6 cm.

What was Gudea's architecture like?
Very little remains of Gudea's works, but there are two huge earthenware cylinders in this room covered in writing that tells how the god Ningirsu inspired the prince to construct a new temple.

◀ *Gudea Cylinder*, ca. 2120 BC.
Moulded earthenware. H. 56.5 cm.

25

Laws predating the Bible

Our knowledge of the cradle of civilisation comes above all from texts engraved in stone discovered in the 19th century. The most important of these stones was the code of the king Hammurabi. The work is not only a code of law, but also a work of history and literature, elegantly relating the society, religion, economy, and laws of Babylon, the capital of Mesopotamia in the 8th century BC.

"I establish truth and justice, I ensure the well-being of the people."

At the top of the stele, the king of Babylon is depicted standing before a bearded god wearing a tiara and sitting on a throne. The king is shown raising a hand to his mouth, a sign of devotion in Mesopotamia. Below the pair, the black stone is covered in a long cuneiform text in the Akkadian language.

Who is this god?
It could be Marduk, the patron deity of Babylon, or Shamash, the sun god and patron deity of Justice.

▶ *Code of Hammurabi,* first half of the 18th century BC. Basalt. H. 2.25 m.

Why is this stele so important?

It is an extraordinary account of the political and social history of a reign during which Babylon took control of Mesopotamia. The stele even became a literary model for schools of scribes over a thousand years. It illustrates the quality of cuneiform writing, which the Babylonians adopted from the Akkadians to transcribe their own language. Their script was made up of about a hundred ideograms; it was however not quite an alphabet.

What does it have to do with our culture?

It is essential because the Hammurabi, of Semitic origin, made a break with Sumerian mentalities to introduce the law of talon, or retaliation, in the Bible: "But if there is harm, then you shall pay life for life, eye for eye, tooth for tooth…"

"Such is the justice that Hammurabi in his competence has established to bind the country to truth, order, and fair-mindedness."

KIDS' CORNER
Don't miss the *Lion's Head*, a copper statue with terrifying eyes. The statue was one of the guardians of the temple of Mari.

▶ *Lion's Head*,
19th century BC.
Copper and incrustations.
38 x 70 cm.

To round off this visit, take a look at case 15, devoted to literary and scientific writing. The rooms of the Louvre's department of Oriental Antiquities contain examples of a range of other ancient writings, leading up to Arabic script. There is also a room devoted to Egyptian writing (see p. 34), and another looking at ancient Greek (Room 2, Denon, lower ground floor).

Egyptian civilisation lasted four thousand years, which were marked by geographical, socio-political, religious and cultural continuity. Spread along the Nile valley, the civilisation was composed of a population of priests, farmers, fishermen, and craftsmen, all subjects of the Pharaoh's powerful regime, held in place by a belief system based on omnipresent gods and an obsession with the afterlife. The Louvre's collection gives you a chance to discover how the Egyptians worked in the fields, reared animals, hunted, and fished. It includes examples of their hieroglyphics, materials and techniques, architecture and furniture, clothing and pastimes, religion and funerary rites, and other aspects of their way of life. It also exhibits some of the masterpieces of their art, which combined realism with idealisation.

THE MYSTERIES OF EGYPT REVEALED BY JEAN-FRANÇOIS CHAMPOLLION (1790-1832)

The Great Sphinx of Tanis

The body of a lion and the head of a Pharaoh - what a strange animal indeed! Throughout the visit, you will encounter a number of hybrid creatures, showing how some animals were sacred and how the Egyptians lived in symbiosis with the animal kingdom. For many centuries the Egyptian civilisation was a total mystery, as impenetrable as its pyramids. Archaeologists only started exploring it in the late 18th century and, in 1820, Champollion, orientalist and creator of the "Egyptian Museum" at the Louvre, managed to decipher hieroglyphics. His discovery has enabled us today to understand the Egyptian religion, as well as their daily life.

Life and Afterlife in Egypt

The Nile, source of life

Egyptian civilisation was concentrated on the banks of the River Nile, which flows from Uganda and Ethiopia through Egypt to form a wide delta before joining the Mediterranean. The Ancient Egyptian year was structured by the river's annual flooding, which brought fertility to the dry desert lands. It was also the main means of communication and transport.

Still waters run deep

In this model dating from 2000 BC, men and women on a boat with masts and canopy are depicted standing around a body, possibly that of a child, swathed in bandages. The body has been mummified and is making the journey to its tomb. In the same case, there are other boats, with oarsmen, and in the furthest case, its owner seems to be holding a flower in his hand.

▲ *Model of Boat*, ca. 2000 BC.
Painted wood. 49 x 77.5 cm. Case 2.

Why go boating with a mummy?
The river was said to separate the world of the living to the east, from the world of the dead to the west where the sun sets. As there were no bridges over the Nile, boats like this one were used at funeral ceremonies to cross the river.

KIDS' CORNER
Make sure you show younger children the Nile wildlife - fish, frogs, crocodiles, hippopotami, and ibises - depicted beneath boats and on the limestone relief featuring a fishing scene, situated on the right-hand wall.

Flooding, germination, and harvest

These three superimposed scenes should be read from bottom to top.
At the bottom, the peasants are seen preparing the earth, turning it ready
for sewing. In the middle, others are seen harvesting with reaping hooks,
while girls gather the harvest. At the top, the ears of corn are carried in baskets
to cattle that trample and thresh the grain. Most neighbouring scenes
also concern agriculture.

▲ *Paintings from the Tomb of Ounsou,* ca. 1450 BC. Painting on silt.
68 x 94 cm. Case 3 on the right, at the entrance.

Who was Ounsou?

Ounsou was the scribe
and grain accountant
at the temple of the god Amun
in Thebes, so was also in charge
of monitoring cereal growing.
There is also a sculpture
of him with his wife,
Imenhetep, in this room.

What crops were grown in Egypt?

Mainly cereals, which formed the basis
of food - such as bread and cakes
- but also a great many vegetables
and fruits.

KIDS' CORNER
Take a look in the Mastaba of Akhethotep.
The reliefs illustrating life on the banks
of the Nile are fascinating.

Earth food

The Egyptian diet was reliant on agriculture, but also on rearing animals, hunting, and fishing. Their diet was not that dissimilar from ours, consisting of bread, wine, and beer staples. We have found out much about their diet from tombs, which have yielded an incredible cross-section of the daily menu of the living, but also an inventory of everything required for continuance in the afterlife.

A feast for eternity

Tepemankh is depicted sitting in front of a table full of slices of bread. Above him, ordered in rows and columns, is a hieroglyphic list of all the food necessary for the survival of the deceased in the afterlife.

Was all this food really placed in the tomb?
Offerings of fresh produce were often used, but the hieroglyphs themselves provided a substitute for real food, which did not keep for long. In this way, the deceased could eat for eternity.

▲ *The menu of Tepemankh,* ca. 2350-2300 BC. Limestone. 1.18 x 1.01 m. Case 5.

KID'S CORNER
Case 9 contains actual food - fruit, grains, fruit stones and even onions!

Bread and beer

This relief shows two bakers at work. The baker on the right is preparing the dough, while his colleague watches over the bread or cakes as they bake.

▶ *The creation and cooking of bread,* 2500-2350 BC. Painted limestone. Case 6.

This wooden model shows three brewers hard at work. Two are crushing the grain, while the work of a third, a woman, seems to have been lost to time. Next to her are an urn and jugs of beer.

◀ *Brewery scene,* 2033-1710 BC. Painted wood. 14.4 x 29.5 x 20.3 cm. Case 6.

Did Egyptian bread look like our own?

Egyptian bread had a more rustic texture and often contained sand. Archaeologists have often noted that the teeth of deceased ancient Egyptian are worn due to the poor quality of the bread. Chunks of bread more than 3500 years old have also been found, and are displayed in the same case. We can only hope there were good dentists in the afterlife.

How did they make beer?

Crushed wheat and barley were used to make a dough that was cooked quickly, then crumbled into an urn of water, and sweetened with dates to aid fermentation. The mixture was then filtered to obtain a strong drink, and stored in urns. The Ancient Egyptians loved their beer. They also produced wine, but this was a luxury drink (see Case 7).

KIDS' CORNER
Case 3 features Ancient Egyptian pets - cats and dogs, but also monkeys. Egypt is in Africa, after all.

Hieroglyphic writing

Hieroglyphic script contains 700 symbols, which were written vertically and horizontally. The symbols are made up of ideograms, phonograms, and determiners. Ideograms are based on pictograms, drawings that represent an object. Phonograms suggest a sound, and sentences of phonograms resemble rebus puzzles; cuneiform writing also worked this way (see p. 23). Determiners are used to indicate the category of word to which they are associated.

"A man who knows how to write"

This statue depicts a scribe with the tools of his trade - palette, jars, and knife - sitting cross-legged with a papyrus on his knees. There is also a letter written on the papyrus, which reads from right to left: "I shall send you the plaintiffs. When they reach you, you shall present them to the god Amun. He shall judge them and shall recognise the liar and the innocent. You shall set the judgement down in writing and bring it to me..."

◀ Scribe sitting cross-legged, ca. 2500-2350 BC. Painted limestone. 58 x 35 cm. Case 1a.

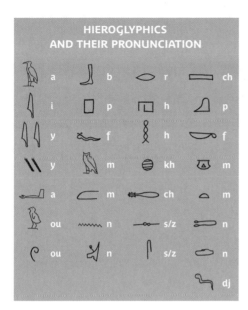

HIEROGLYPHICS
AND THEIR PRONUNCIATION

(chart of hieroglyphic symbols with pronunciations: a, b, r, ch, i, p, h, p, y, f, h, f, y, m, kh, m, a, m, ch, m, ou, n, s/z, n, ou, n, s/z, n, dj)

Was writing in hieroglyphics difficult?

Only scribes who trained for years were able to master the symbols. There were three different ways of writing - neat, detailed hieroglyphs, neat cursive hieroglyphs, and highly simplified cursive hieroglyphs - and over time the original symbols became increasingly harder to recognise.

What is papyrus?

Papyrus is a water plant with fibrous stalks. Ancient Egyptians used it to make a form of paper, like we use wood-fibre today. Other supports were also used for writing: wood, earthenware, wood, and parchment.

Must try harder!

On this tablet is written the first phrase of a "school book", containing a collection of stock phrases for letters that was studied and copied by apprentice scribes. The word *kemit* means "amount". The signs are poorly written, and there are mistakes, the work of a pupil who really must try harder.

What does the text mean?

This particular excerpt means: "A slave says to his master that he wishes him life, health, strength and eternity, for always, in accordance with the wishes of this humble servant." In the same case there are examples of documentary, religious, and literary texts.

▲ *Pupil's tablet/kemit,*
ca. 1963-1650 BC.
Stuccoed wood. Case 4.

A civilisation of craftsmen

Not all Egyptians were farmers. Many were specialised in crafts. Manufacturing daily objects, and constructing houses and furniture, required many hands.

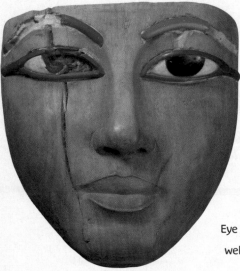

As though alive!

This magnificent face is reminiscent of queen Nefertiti herself. The face's fine features are enhanced by incrustations in the wood of the coffin. The eyes are made-up, as was customary in Egypt. Eye make-up was used to look elegant as well as to protect the eyes from the sun.

◄ *Wooden coffin with glass eyes, ca. 1400-1300 BC. Case 11.*

What are the eyes made of?
The eyes are made of glass-paste, a material that cost less than precious stones, which were the preserve of only the richest. Glassmakers were able to craft glass into all kinds of forms, using a whole range of colours.

What materials did craftsmen use?
Craftsmen used materials that were commonplace in Egypt, such as stone for sculptures, clay for pottery, wood and palm leaves, but also materials imported from very far away, like gold and ebony from other parts of Africa, lapis-lazuli from Afghanistan, or cedar wood from the Lebanon.

▲ *Furniture*, the central case of Room 8.

A familiar setting

A house's basic furnishings were composed of an assortment of baskets, chests, seats, headrests, mats and fabrics, made of wood, straw, esparto grass and palm leaves. Unfortunately there are few remains of houses that were constructed of pisé, a mixture of clay and plant matter. However in funerary rites, Egyptians liked to surround themselves with pictures or effigies of their homes, and these remnants have survived to the present day.

Far from exotic

Egyptian furnishings looked much like our own, and could easily come from the countryside today. However, in those days, the beds were probably not as comfortable.

KIDS' CORNER
Have a look in Case 3
at the tiny models of houses.

Refined society

Finery and toilette played an important role in Egyptian society, at least for those who could afford such things. Egyptian jewellery was of high quality, and appears surprisingly refined and delicate today. Luxury clothing and beauty products were also made of refined, quality materials. The richer inhabitants of the Nile's banks were also fond of concerts, theatre, and parlour games.

Mirror, mirror, on the wall...

This pleated linen dress has been conserved intact, and is presented among a whole host of extraordinary jewellery and ornamentation made of gold, precious stones, pearls, and shells, and decorated with animal or plant motifs, hieroglyphics, and royal insignia. On the other side of the room there are mirrors, bottles of kohl (the black eye-liner), and make-up scoops.

▶ *Pleated dress*, 2033-1710 BC, 121 x 57 cm. Case 4.

Was this dress worn everyday?
Given the refinement of the pleats, it must have been a ceremonial costume, like those worn during religious festivals or to concerts.

Did everyone wear make-up?

No, but among the upper classes, men and women alike took great care of their appearance. The black eyeliner "kohl" was often worn to enhance the eyes and protect them from the sun and illness.

What were the scoops for?

Certainly not for food, but instead for creating the mixes necessary for creating make-up. These scoops were the most refined objects of an Egyptian's toilette, and a pretext for adding great realism to reconstructions today.

KIDS' CORNER: THE GAME OF THE GOOSE

In Case 8 there is a rather unusual hippopotamus with 58 evenly spaced holes in his back, into which the Egyptians placed jackal-headed sticks. Now there's a funny game!

How was it played?

The game is a precursor to the Game of the Goose, which later became Snakes and Ladders. Players throw dice or cast knucklebones, and moved their "counters" round the "board". Some holes meant players skipped forward a hole, while others sent players back.

▲ *Playing board of 58 holes in the shape of a hippopotamus,*
ca. 664-332 BC. Siliceous faience with inset glass.
7.4 x 21.5 x 18 cm. Case 8.

▶▶ *Ancient Egypt was a civilisation of relentless builders, and Room 11 gives a hint of Egyptians' impressive command of architecture. While the Pyramids are the best-known example, this civilisation also produced temples, necropolises, and palaces. It has been possible to transport some smaller pieces to Paris, such as the obelisk from Luxor on the Place de la Concorde, a gift from Egypt to France in the 19th century. This room also exhibits a number of sphinxes, which, like the obelisks, symbolically protected temples.*

The gods' abode

Gods played an essential role in Egyptian daily life.
They were served by a large clergy and embodied
in the pharaoh, or took on animal forms; Egyptian gods
were considered to be living beings. Their temples
are full-scale palaces, entry to which was forbidden
to mortals

Oh heavens! What big feet you have!

The colossal scale of temple architecture can be gauged from the size of
the granite feet from a broken statue exhibited in this room, as well as from
the columns of pink granite behind. Unlike human houses, the dwellings
of the gods were built of stone, and must have been pretty impressive.

▼ *Feet of a royal colossus inscribed by Amenophis III,*
ca. 1391-1353 BC. Granite. 1.53 x 2.25 x 1.44 m.

Where are the feet from?
From the funerary temple
of the pharaoh Amenophis III
in Thebes, today's Luxor, home
to the most beautiful surviving
Egyptian temples. It is as though
the subjugated people parading
on the base are being crushed
by the feet.

An extraordinary divine bestiary

While the sphinx has a human head and an animal body, elsewhere in this room there are a number of human bodies bearing animal heads: Sekhmet with the head of a lioness at the entrance of the room, Menthu with a bulls head (Case 3), Hathor with a cow's head. Some gods though manage to keep up appearances, such as Amun, the great sun-god.

◄ *The ram-god Khnum.*
Quartzite. 126 x 35 x 99 cm.

KIDS' CORNER
At the top of all Egyptian columns there are decorations, called capitals. Some capitals are shaped like palm trees (**palmiform**); others look like the papyrus (**papyriform**); others are like lotus flowers (**lotiform**); and others have the head of the cow-goddess Hathor (**hathoric**) as in the next room. The cow-goddess was a goddess of protection. See if you can find any other half-human, half-animal figures in these rooms.

palmiform

papyriform

lotiform

hathoric

The great journey

The land of the living was only separated from that of the dead by the Nile, but the journey the living had to take to reach the afterlife was much more than a simple ferry crossing. Everybody had to make ready for the adventure - according to their economic means, of course. While pharaohs enjoyed the prospect of a colossal pyramid, lowlier citizens could look forward to a hole in the desert sand. No matter the size, the tomb was your home for eternity.

A family reunited

In this crypt, similar to royal tombs, the goddess Isis uses the wind from her wings to breath vitality into her brother, the god Osiris, sovereign of the kingdom of the Dead.

Why is Osiris so important for pharaohs' tombs?
After their death, the now deified kings were said to join Osiris in the kingdom of the Dead, extending their majesty to into eternity. Osiris, killed by his brother Set, was brought back to life by his sister, who bore his child, the sky-god Horus, whose eyes were believed to be the sun and moon.

What is that enormous sarcophagus in the middle of the crypt?
It is the sarcophagus of Ramses III from his tomb in the Valley of the Kings. His mummy was retrieved intact from it, and is now conserved in the Cairo Museum. The sarcophagus weighs 18 tons!

▲ *Isis spreads her wings to protect Osiris*, ca. 945-715 BC. Bronze, formerly partly gold. H. 20.5 cm. Case 8.

Russian Dolls?

The Louvre contains a remarkable collection of sarcophagi, which are indicative of the Egyptians' concern for the preservation of their mortal form for eternity. The set of sarcophagi stack inside each other, and form a solid and ornate protection for the mummified body.

Who was Tamutneferet?

Tamutneferet was a priestess of the god Amun and held a very important position in the Egyptian priesthood. She was clearly very wealthy as these painted wooden sarcophagi show. Their decoration features a whole host of magical formulae and prayers to gods to protect her on the long journey. Most Egyptians were entombed in a single wooden casket.

▶ *Sarcophagi of Lady Tamutneferet,* ca. 1295-1186 BC. Treated, gilded and painted wood. 180 x 48 cm.

KIDS' CORNER
Look at the disproportionate sizes of the heads on the stone sarcophagi on each side of the staircase.

43

The palace of the mummy

Tombs were meant to be replicas of the living world, so they have greatly helped us understand the daily life and customs of the Ancient Egyptian people. We have even been able to study their corpses. Egyptians embalmers, under the gaze of the jackal-god Anubis, were remarkably specialised in their art.

▲ *Mummy of a Man with Cartonnages,* ca. 3rd-2nd century BC. Linen, painted and plastered linen. L. 1.67 m. Case 1.

Perfect conservation, or almost...

Here is an anonymous mummy, wrapped in its linen bandages and protected by its plastered and painted linen covers, known as "cartonnages". The case shows all the instruments necessary for embalming.

How were bodies embalmed?

First bodies were treated with natron, a resin salt and oils. The entrails were placed into special recipients, known as "canopic jars". The body was then wrapped in linen bandages and protective cartonnages, and placed in a sarcophagus. Only luxury embalming was capable of preserving a body intact for over four thousand years. Another mummy, without wrappings, is conserved in the Roman Egypt rooms (Room A, Denon, lower ground floor).

The tomb is a refuge for the body of the deceased and its home for eternity. The architecture and furnishings of tombs depended on the social rank, and offer insights into the changing ideas about life after death in every period. Case 3 contains the funerary furniture of the Chancellor Nakhti, whose statue is in Room 23 on the 1st floor.

▲ *Contents of a tomb in Room 16*

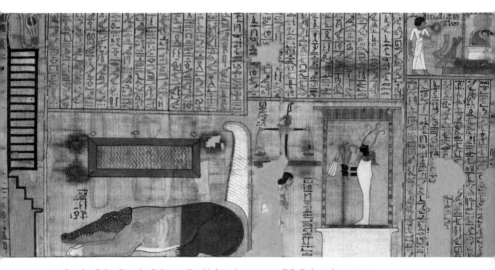

▲ *Book of the Dead of the scribe Nebqed,* ca. 1400 BC. Painted papyrus. H. 30 cm (approx.). Case 2, Room 17.

The Book of the Dead

Actually a long papyrus, the so-called Book of the Dead was conserved rolled up. The scroll is covered with hieroglyphics and reads from left to right. There are also illustrations relating to funerary rites, and above all, the transition from one world to the next, the most important moment of which was the "heart weighing" ceremony prior to entering the kingdom of Osiris.

What is written in the book?
The text contains a collection of magical formulae enabling access to the world of the dead; it is effectively a "passport" to the beyond. Also known as "The Book of Coming Forth by Day", it enabled the deceased to retain freedom of movement. Its longest version contains 165 chapters.

45

A pantheon of all shapes and sizes

The Egyptian religion had a countless number of divinities. There were the higher gods, such as the god Amun, and more mundane deities, like the many protective spirits. There were even some animal gods.

The dictionary of the gods

What a gawky body and what a fiendish face! Call that a god? It looks more like some hideous monster or evil troll.

Why is Bes so ugly?
Appearances can be deceptive. Bes is in fact a god of protection, and is supposed to scare off the forces of evil. He brings joy through music, and even watches over dreams. Case 1 shows most of the Egyptian gods, and gives details about their respective attributes, as well as the different forms they took, whether human or animal.

▸ *The God Bes,* ca. 379-341 BC. Limestone. 92 x 62 x 28.5 cm.

A sort of "Noah's Ark"

Case 19 contains mummified animals of all kinds, ranging from the shrew to the crocodile, with cats, dogs, ibises, fish, falcons, scarab beetles, and even snakes. All these animals were sacred and each one associated with a god. Hence, like humans, they were carefully protected in linen bandages before being placed in sarcophagi.

▸ *Mummy of a cat.* Case 8, Room 19.

Why were animals mummified?

The mummification of animals showed their importance in a world where spirituality was an essential part of daily life. The former world of the deceased was reconstructed in the tomb, ready for the afterlife, and eternity would have been a sad place without pets or sacred animals. Even larger animals like Apis bulls and rams were mummified.

KID'S CORNER: A FEW GODS

Anubis   Bastet   Hathor   Horus

Maat   Ptah   Thoth

To find out more about the life in ancient Egypt, make sure you visit the rooms on the first floor where the finest of Egyptian art is exhibited. You may like to finish with the rooms devoted to Coptic Egypt and Roman Egypt (Denon, lower ground floor, Room A) where a mummy is exhibited without wrappings, with marvellous painted portraits of the Fayoum oasis.

PRACTICAL INFO
From the Pyramid, head towards the Denon wing, to the lower ground floor and turn left straight away into the rooms devoted to pre-classical Greece. These lead to the ground floor where the sculpture rooms are to be found. The tour continues up to the first floor of the Sully wing, where you will find examples of splendidly illustrated Greek ceramics, alongside examples of skilled metalwork, from weaponry to jewellery. On the way, you will come across the famous **Winged Victory of Samothrace,** *as well as masterpieces of Greek sculpture like the* **Venus de Milo,** *and a fragment of the frieze of the Parthenon (which is currently in a temporary location, due to refurbishment of the Greek sculpture rooms).*

Ancient Greece is the place of origin of modern Western civilisation. It developed its key aspects during the early Aegean civilisation, which include a belief system based on divine mythology, a culture born of Homeric verse, and a political structure in the form of the city-state. Athens subsequently became the heart of Greek civilisation and its zenith came in the 5th century BC with Pericles and the triumph of democracy. In the 4th century, Alexander extended the Greek empire to the Indus. First, let us take a look at their gods and heroes.

ENTER GODS AND HEROES
Black-figure Attic dinos by the painter of the Gorgon, ca. 580 BC. Room 1.

This spectacular vase displays a decor of plant designs and real and imaginary animals. However, the focal points of the dinos are on either side: firstly, the combat opposing two heavily armed hoplite soldiers, sandwiched between two chariots, symbolic of the wars which divided Greek cities; and secondly, the hero Perseus, son of Zeus, fleeing the monstrous Gorgons, who are angry that he cut off the head of their sister Medusa; Hermes and Athena look on. Greek heroes are often the offspring of gods and mortals, so they have an important role to play in Greek religion. Hermes and Athena were also the offspring of Zeus; Hermes was Zeus's messenger and the god of trade and thieves; while Athena was the patron-god of Athens, the goddess of wisdom, but also of war.

Greece, the birth of a civilisation

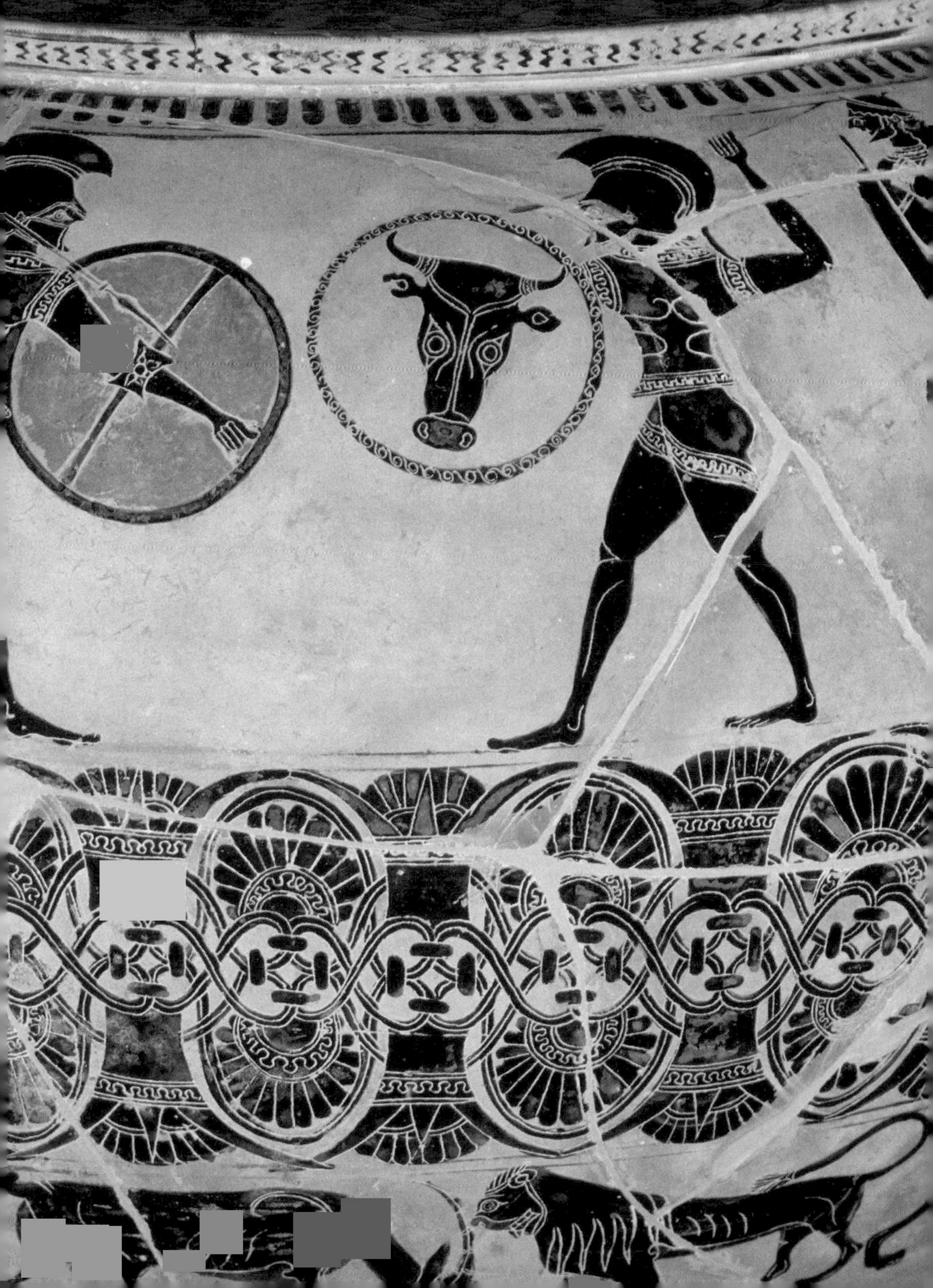

The dawn of culture

In Greek mythology, the giant Prometheus created the first man, modelling him from clay; he then stole Zeus's fire. Prometheus was punished for this audacious act, but was finally freed by Heracles. The Greeks believed that they were created in the image of their gods, so always depicted them in ideal forms.

Athenian nobility

Among the many headless sculptures in this room this sculpture of the head of a young horseman, with his gentle smile and carefully braided curls and beard, cuts a fine figure. Unlike the rigid frontal pose of the other statues in the room, the young man seems to twist slightly to his left.

Who is the handsome rider?
He is believed to be a young Athenian aristocrat, and the crown of foliage suggests that he is an Olympic champion; the Olympic games were created in 776 BC. Sporting events and competitions gave Greek cities the chance to confront each other without fighting, and also to celebrate a common culture.

▲ *Head of a Horseman*, known as the *Rampin Horseman*, ca. 550 BC. Island marble. H. 27 cm (head only).

Why is this statue called a "head"?

Originally exhibited alone, the head was later matched with the torso of the rider and the neck of the horse, which are conserved separately in Athens, and have been copied to complement the Louvre head. The group is one of the oldest known equestrian statues.

▶▶ *Room 2 is devoted to the study of Greek writings about institutions, public life, culture, and education.*

Virility and power

The slight curve and twist of the body endows this torso of a man with a sense of power. The musculature is meticulously rendered, and the dark marble adds to the feeling of density.

Is this work realistic?

Not at all, even if the sculptor did call on a particularly muscular model. The "kouros" is an allegory, the vision of an ideal form, called a "canon", which was used to represent gods and heroes, like the "korai" represented an ideal feminine form. It is believed that this is a statue of Apollo, the god of arts and beauty.

Why is he naked?

For the Greeks, virile nudity was customary. Athletes would train and compete naked. Gods and heroes were also depicted in the simplest clothing, which glorified the physical qualities of man, and conveyed him in the image of the gods.

▸ *Male Torso*, known as the *Miletus Torso*, ca. 480-470 BC. Marble. H. 1.32 m.

Masterly art

The 5th century was the pinnacle of the Greek
civilisation in Athens when Pericles founded
a new political system, democracy,
which questioned the aristocracy's
exclusive power. Pericles constructed
huge temples, the most famous of
which is the Parthenon in the heart
of the Acropolis. Through the chisels
of Phidias or Polykleitos, sculpture
became a model for centuries
to come, forming the basis
of "Classicism".

A hero at work

The theme of the decorative cycle
in the temple of Olympus is the
twelve tasks of Heracles (or
"Hercules" for the Romans) and
is a perfect example of classical
Greek sculpture. A scale model
of a Doric-style temple gives
a clear idea of the importance
of this monumental temple
dedicated to Zeus, whose gigantic
statue of the god in gold and ivory
was considered one of the Seven
Wonders of the World. Heracles is
here depicted wrestling with the
fearsome bull of King Minos, as he
attempts to tame it. This was the
seventh of his twelve tasks.

Who was Heracles?
Heracles was the son of Zeus and Alcmene,
a mortal. He was visited by two nymphs
who offered him a choice between a life
of vice or virtue. Heracles chose virtue and
devoted his life to its glory. Later the jealous
goddess Hera drove Heracles to madness,
and he killed his wife and children.
To expiate the crimes, he was set twelve
labours. After his death, Heracles entered
Olympus, the world of the gods.

Why does Heracles have to catch the bull?
The sea-god Poseidon asked the King Minos
of Crete to sacrifice the bull, but Minos
decided to spare it. Poseidon was furious,
and goaded the animal to destroy the island
of Crete. As one of his twelve labours,
Heracles had to tame the bull, a deed
of which only a true hero was capable.

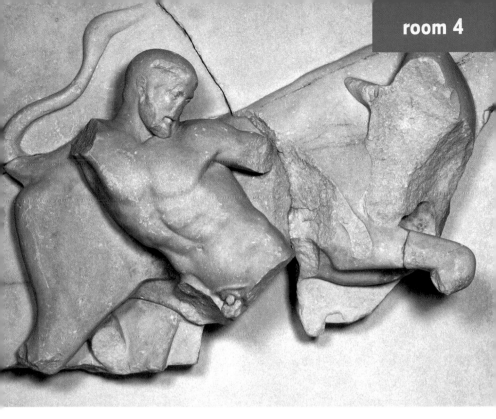

▲ Fourth western metope, Temple of Olympus: *Heracles and the Cretan Bull*, ca. 460 BC. Paros marble. 1.14 x 1.52 m.

What is a metope?

A metope is a feature of a Doric frieze in a temple. A metope of the Doric frieze of the Parthenon can be seen in the next room (the Salle de Diane), showing a centaur attempting to abduct a woman. Some friezes were continuous, like the Ionic frieze of the Parthenon, a fragment of which is presented in Room 6 (see pp. 54-55).

THE CAPITALS

Doric   **Ionic**   **Corinthian**

KIDS' CORNER
See what capitals you can find in the Louvre's architecture.

▲ The so-called *Panel of the Ergastines* from the Parthenon frieze,
ca. 440 BC. Marble. 96 x 207 cm.

Grace and femininity

Six young women of the Athenian
aristocracy and two priests
(regrettably lacking their heads) are
seen taking part in the Panatheneia
procession, which took place in
Athens every four years, in honour
of the goddess Athena. The six
"Ergastines" are dressed in long
draped robes. Originally, the
background of this frieze was blue,
and the bodies were enhanced
in gold.

What was the celebration for?

The procession was both a civil
and religious celebration in homage
to the patron-goddess of the town,
at which sports, poetry, and music
competitions were staged. The whole
population would take part,
as represented on this long frieze
running round the temple's colonnade.
For the festival, young noble women
would traditionally weave a huge robe
to dress the 12-metre high statue
of Athena. The temple itself is colossal:
70 x 30 metres.

Was nudity reserved for men?

Yes, with the exception of goddesses, and in particular Aphrodite (Venus), goddess of beauty and love. In the rather macho Mediterranean world, female mortals could not be seen naked.

Goddess of love

The model of Aphrodite naked is a copy of the work of one of the greatest 4th-century Athenian sculptors, Praxiteles. The head combines grace and majesty, illustrating an ideal of femininity and divinity.

▲ *Aphrodite*, known as the *"Kaufmann Head"*, 2nd century BC. Marble. H. 35 cm.

▶▶ *As you climb the large Daru staircase, you pass in front of the* Winged Victory *of Samothrace (see p. 9). A little further in the Salle des Sept Cheminées, you will find the* Venus de Milo, *a canon of feminine beauty from the Hellenist era, displayed in its temporary exhibition space (see p. 8). Next we enter the rooms of the Charles X museum, containing small terracotta works, and above all painted ceramics. Don't forget to look up and admire the ceilings.*

The painting of history and mythology

Our knowledge about Greek painting comes from ceramic vases. These vases also illustrate Greek mythology and history, alongside scenes of daily life. Room 39 includes a selection of vases by theme: Olympian gods, the heroes Theseus and Heracles, the Trojan War, the tragedies, athletics, love and the feminine world, funerary rites, and banquets.

The king of the gods

Zeus, god of the sky and master of Olympus, is shown in red against a black background with his traditional attributes: the eagle and the thunderbolt. The eagle was just one of the forms that Zeus took during his adventures, along with that of a swan, white bull, or golden rain.

▲ *Red-figure Amphora: Zeus,* ca. 480-470 BC, H. 31 cm. Case 1.

What were Zeus's adventures?
Zeus was notoriously unfaithful to his wife, Hera, and he loved disguising himself to seduce mortals, both female and male - the most famous of whom was the youth Ganymede. From his couplings with mortal women the god had many children: either gods like Apollo, Dionysos (Case 2), and Athena, or heroes such as Heracles (Cases 4 and 5), Perseus, and the twins Castor and Pollux.

How did Zeus use thunderbolts?

The thunderbolt was a weapon created by his uncles, the Cyclopes, to lighten up the sky. While they were deemed an awesome manifestation of the god's anger, they guaranteed the survival of mankind by bringing "god-sent rain" for the crops.

Did the Trojan War actually take place?

On the belly of this vase we see Achilles, a main protagonist of the Trojan Wars, receiving his weapons from a group of women, while on the left he is depicted naked preparing to don his armour and helmet. The black figures stand out like shadow-puppets against the light background.

▲ *Black figure Hydria: arming Achilles,* ca. 575-550 BC. H. 38.3 cm. Case 6.

What role did Achilles play in the war?

Homer recounts the exploits of the Greek hero in the Illiad. The war was started by Paris, son of Priam, the king of Troy, who kidnapped the beautiful Helen, wife to the Spartan king, Menelaus. To avenge the outrage, the Greeks were led by Agamemnon, the brother of Menelaus and king of Mycenae. The Greek army was packed with heroes: Achilles, king of the Myrmidons, his friend Patroclus, his cousin Ajax, and Ulysses, king of Ithaca, to name but a few; in the Trojan ranks, Hector was the key figure. Few survived the war, however. Homer's *Odyssey* relates the fall of Troy and the adventures of Ulysses on the return journey to Ithaca.

Birth of a myth: King Oedipus

This creature with the bust of a woman and the body of a lion and wings of a bird is as surprising to us today as the Egyptians' Sphinx.

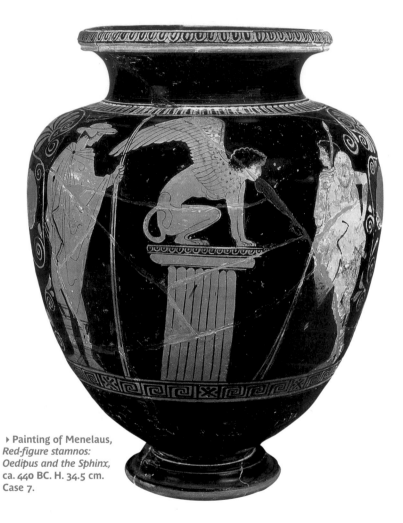

▸ Painting of Menelaus,
Red-figure stamnos:
Oedipus and the Sphinx,
ca. 440 BC. H. 34.5 cm.
Case 7.

What is the meaning of this myth?

The monster was sent by Hera to terrorise the inhabitants of the island of Boeotia, until they found the answer to her riddle: "What is the creature that walks on four legs in the morning, two legs at noon and three in the evening?" Oedipus's answer was "man" and he escaped death. See if you can work out why.

Artists, the "photographers" of their age

In Greek civilisation, the division of the sexes was very marked. To men were reserved war, sport, and pleasure. Women's role was much more peaceful in comparison. Their role as wife and mother was highly respected in domestic life, and they were allotted their own private "apartment" in their homes, the *gynaecium*.

The athlete, the paragon of virtue

A naked athlete prepares to cast the discus. We can imagine him training at the palestra (gym) or competing in huge stadiums in sporting events, held during religious festivals.

What sporting disciplines were practised in Greece?
Mainly athletics, such as racing, discus, javelin, long jump, chariot racing, wrestling, and boxing.

▸ *Red-figure cup: discus-thrower,* ca. 490 BC. D. 23 cm. W. 30.5 cm. Case 9.

Was it uniquely a man's world?
Women were not admitted within the enclosure of the Olympic Games. Athletes would rub olive oil and sand into their bodies and would use a small vase, called an aryballos, and a strigil (scraper) to clean themselves after competition. Athletes were drawn from the upper classes of Greek society. They were considered as models of perfection and honoured as heroes.

The mysterious world of women

Here is a group of women
of differing ages, depicted
calmly going about their daily
tasks and grooming
in their apartments.

**Were men allowed
in the *gynaecium*?**

Not in principle, just as men are
not allowed into the harem in Muslim
countries. Women were not confined
indoors however, even they were rarely
involved in the intellectual and political
life of the country.

▲ *Black figure amphora: gynaecium,*
ca. 520-510 BC. 25 cm. Case 11.

Did men have greater freedom?

Yes. They were also free to exploit their slaves and have relations
with other men (Case 10).

KID'S CORNER

The gallery made up of rooms devoted
to ceramics is like a huge story-book full of Greek
mythological heroes, like Heracles. In the parallel
gallery, the Charles X Museum, are displayed some
marvellous terracotta figurines, the equivalent
of dolls in Antiquity. In a display case in Room 36,
see if you can find a game of knucklebones hidden
in the neck of a figurine of Heracles.

Weaponry and jewellery

The Greeks' command of metalwork was astounding, and the weapons and daily objects they produced are impressive. Again, their metalwork reveals the division of the sexes in Greek society.

Armed to the teeth

This helmet is similar to those that feature on the vases depicting the exploits of Greek warriors, and is almost contemporary to the works of Homer. It perfectly covers the nose and cheeks and must have made the hoplites, or Greek foot-soldiers, look terrifying. A Greek soldier's equipment included weapons, armour, shield, and other diverse forms of bodily protection.

▲ *Corinthian-style helmet, 7th century BC. Bronze. Case M3.*

The symbol of victory

The crown of laurels was one of Apollo's hallmarks. It was the symbol of victory, but also poetry, and the winners of Olympic events wore it with pride. In the Middle Ages, university scholars were crowned with laurel wreaths of leaves and berries, *bacca laurea*, which gave us the word "baccalaureate".

▲ *Crown of laurel leaves and berries, end 5th-4th century BC. Gold. Diam. 2.5 cm.*

▸▸ *Before going down into the Salle des Cariatides (Room 16) by the Henri II staircase, stop for a moment in front of the gilded bronze statue of Apollo discovered in Lillebonne, in Normandy. It is a reminder that original Greek statues were mainly sculpted in metal; marble was only used to make copies. In the staircase, look up to appreciate the Renaissance decoration and ornate H of Henri II.*

A people of marble

The last period of Greek civilisation, called the Hellenistic period, stretched from the 4th to the 1st century BC. This was the era of Alexander the Great and of Cleopatra, when Greek civilisation had a huge influence on the Mediterranean area as well as to the east, an influence that endured until the Roman conquest. Democracy was replaced by the monarchy, and new metropolises such as Alexandria and Pergamum became the jewels in the crown of the Mediterranean.

The Salle des Cariatides was once the reception room of the palace of François I, and is a masterpiece of Renaissance architecture. The musicians' gallery is supported by the room's famous caryatids, formed by columns of female figures. The room now houses Hellenistic sculpture, a freer development of Classicism, which produced a number of masterpieces (see pp. 8 and 9). Look out for Diane of Versailles, and the hybrid creatures such as the centaurs and the hermaphrodite, a creature that was half-woman, half-man.

The cult of great men

While some heroes are imaginary, some really did exist, like Alexander the Great (356-323 BC), son of Philip, king of Macedonia. Alexander was one of Antiquity's great conquerors, and the role-model for France's Louis XIV.

Is this a genuine portrait?
Not in the way we understand portraiture today, particularly because it is a late copy. However, it is one of the very rare portraits of a Greek sovereign we have inherited.

▸ *Portrait of Alexander the Great, know as Hermes Azara, 1st-2nd century AD. Pentelic marble. H. 68 cm.*

The adventures of a Gaul in Greece

Here we see a courageous warrior defending himself to the death, the wound on the left leg is however a clear indication that he is in difficulty. The statue is a perfect illustration of Hellenistic Greek art, known for its highly expressive realism. The warrior's taught muscles, the expression of his face, and his tousled hair, are a far cry from the representation of classical heroes.

‹ *Wounded Gaul,*
1st-2nd century. Alabaster.
97 x 75 x 52 cm.

A Gaul in Greece? How come?

This statue is testimony to the war between the early French and the Greeks. The Ancient Greek civilisation formed colonies along the coastline of what later became France, in particular in Massalia, around 600 BC; today Massalia is Marseille. Migrant Celts from this area, called Galatians by the Greeks, invaded Greece around 280 BC, but were beaten at Kaikos by the king of Pergamum. This sculpture was taken from a monument the king produced to commemorate the victory.

To prolong your visit, you might like to visit the Etruscan and Roman rooms, where the Greek influence can be seen everywhere. You will also find a host of Greek heroes in Classical and Neoclassical paintings, in particular by David (Daru Gallery, Denon wing, Room 75).

PRACTICAL INFO
From the Pyramid, enter the museum through the Denon wing. On the lower ground floor, turn left and go through the rooms devoted to the origins of Greek civilisation, which was one of the models of the Roman civilisation. Then turn right into the first room of Etruscan Antiquities (Room 18), before starting the visit of Roman antiquities via Room 22 (see floor plans).

According to legend, Rome was found by Romulus in 753 BC, and over time the city became the centre of a huge empire. The Roman civilisation was first a kingdom, then a republic from 509 to 27 BC, and finally an empire, which lasted until the 5th century. Rome was always home to a wide range of religions but officially became Christian in the 4th century. The Louvre conserves testaments to many famous Roman figures, together with portrayals of Roman lifestyle and culture, a culture in which the individual had an important place. The sculptures, mosaics, painting, and metalwork in silver and gold that have survived reveal much about the political organisation and the refinement of daily life in ancient Rome.

CHRONOLOGY (MAIN DATES)
509 BC: start of the Roman Republic
ca. 450 BC: the Celts settle in Gaul
52 BC: Vercingetorix is beaten by Julius Caesar at Alesia
27 BC: Augustus founds the Roman Empire
2nd century AD: height of the Roman Empire
476 AD: end of the Roman Empire

ITALY BEFORE ROME
Sarcophagus of a married couple, ca. 590 BC. Room 18.

The tenderness of the couple's pose and their smiles make this sepulchre the living image of a couple joined for eternity. The man and woman are rendered with equal detail, which was not always the case. Inspired by archaic Greek models, this sarcophagus was made at the same time as the fall of the last Etruscan kings and the establishment of the Roman Republic (509 BC), a political system styled on that of Athens. Italy as we know it today was home to a whole range of peoples, including the Etruscans, who originated in Tuscany, an area that the Latins federated in the 5th century BC.

Rome,
from Republic
to Empire

A republic and citizens

The Roman Republic (509-27 BC) was modelled on the Greek example of Pericles's Athens. Society was ruled by its cives, or citizens, an upper class of patrician families who held the Senate, which governed the people, or plebeians. At the lowest end of the scale came the slaves, who had no civic rights whatever.

▲ *Relief of "Domitius Ahenobarbus"*, late 2nd century BC. Marble. L. 2.05 m.

Each citizen in his place

What is happening here? Who are these people?

Featured from left to right: a registrar sitting on a stool, recording a declaration of revenues ❶; a citizen with receipts ❷; two citizens in discussion as they await their turn ❸ (all dressed in straight togas); two soldiers with Greek helmets ❹ standing back to back - one observing the registrar at work, the other watching the scene at the centre of the relief; two musicians ❺ accompanying the god of war, Mars ❻, in battle uniform, standing beside a sacrificial altar at the centre of the composition. On the other side of the altar is a magistrate ❼ who is set to preside over the ceremony, escorted by a page ❽; then, there are slaves ❾ leading three animals (a bull, a ram, and a pig) to slaughter; finally, soldiers and a cavalier ❿ bring up the rear.

What does this scene represent?

Every five years, Roman citizens had to declare their income in a citywide census. The evaluation of individuals' fortunes determined into which of the five classes of the army they would be attributed. This is oldest known Roman historical relief; there is another in the next room, the fragment of the *Ara Pacis Augustae* commemorating the victorious return of Augustus from Gaul and Spain and the return of peace.

Why a sacrifice in honour of Mars?

It was a purification rite. The blood of sacrificed animals was said to redeem the misdeeds of the community. The ceremony took place at the end of the census. The people would thus thank Mars, the god of war, for his help and protection, even in times of peace.

Why the use of marble?

The relief was created just after Rome had conquered Greece. A number of Greek artists settled in Rome and produced works on Roman civic themes, while conserving their preferred materials.

▲ *Portrait of a man,*
ca. 30-25 BC. Bronze. H. 38 cm.

€ach to his own face

The nose is aquiline, the chin slightly receding, the gaze absent, the mouth fine, the hair short and virile, cut well above the ears. Take a look at the other portraits in the same room and you will notice that each one has quite distinct traits and facial expressions. Here, the dominant features are gravitas and determination.

Why all the portraits?

Portraiture is characteristic of the Roman religion. Citizens would commission a sculpted portrait in their lifetime, or their children commissioned one using wax moulds from the deceased's face. The portrait was then placed near the altar of the household gods, the protectors of family life. The way we use photographs today is similar.

▲ Republican portraits, Room 22.

KID'S CORNER
Take a close look at the portraits, their haircuts and beards, and the expressions on their faces.

Did everybody have a portrait?

No, only those rich enough could afford a sculptor to create a portrait in their lifetime. This is one aspect that made the Romans distinct from the Greeks, whose real physiognomy we shall never know. The bronze portrait here is particularly luxurious; other portraits were simply made of clay.

The imperial family

When he took on the title of Emperor Augustus
in 27 BC, Octavius, Julius Caesar's successor, founded
a new political organisation, the Empire. Under Augustus,
Romans enjoyed a long period of peace and prosperity,
after a series of terrible civil wars. The Empire created
by Augustus also left the way open for the abuse
of power.

Augustus, master of the world

The head is slightly inclined, turned to the right
like the statue just behind, and the face is wide
and flat, with high cheekbones, a firm chin, and
a well-defined mouth. It is an official portrait,
with the elegance of a Greek work, but with
the expression of a Roman portrait.

▶ *Bust of the Emperor Augustus,*
ca. the Christian era. Marble. H. 36 cm.

**What were these statues
and busts used for?**

They were used to relay the portrait
of the emperor throughout his empire,
from Britain to Egypt, from North
Africa to India. This also applied
to portraits of the emperor's family,
examples of which can be seen in this
room. Essentially, they were a form
of propaganda.

**Why did the artist focus so intensely
on facial expression?**

Artists will have wanted to demonstrate
the serene yet anxious character of
their reformist ruler, who was also head
of the Empire's armies. In the furrowed
brow there is also a hint of sadness;
Augustus was in his sixties and his
grandsons and heirs were dead.

69

Women's place

With her frosty beauty and elegance, the princess predominates over the woman in this stylised official portrait. The hairstyle, with its curled-back fringe at the front and chignon at the nape, was highly fashionable in the 1st century BC. Both female and male portraits display a wide range of hairstyles in the Roman rooms.

▶ *Empress Livia,* ca. 31 BC. Diorite. H. 32 cm.

Who is she?

Livia was Emperor Augustus's second wife, and the mother of Tiberius. While women could not hold a position of power, they held an important place in the imperial family, particularly as mothers of the successors to the imperial throne.

The material is very different to the customary marble. What is it?

The bust is sculpted from diorite, a very costly stone, probably imported from Egypt at the time of the battle of Actium (31 BC). It was at the battle of Actium that Augustus, who was then still known as Octavius, beat Antony and Cleopatra's flotilla, and assured his place as the successor to Julius Caesar.

▶ *Ceiling of the Salle des Saisons,* by Romanelli, 17th century.

KID'S CORNER

Take a look at the ceiling painting of the Salle des Saisons and try and find the strange sculpted creatures that are half-man, half-goat. This room was once part of the apartments of Queen Anne of Austria, mother of Louis XIV, which were decorated in the 17th century by Italian artists.

The Greek heritage

Here we see a life-size statue of a naked man, sculpted in the finest Greek marble. His face is young and serious, the portrait of a sensitive man placed on an ideal body, the expression of the canon of Greek art. This effigy has a monumental character to it, and is very unlike the private portraits.

Who is this youth?
This is Marcellus, Augustus's son-in-law. The melancholy in the portrait of Augustus (p. 69) is perhaps because of Marcellus, whom Augustus had designated as heir to the throne; alas, the man died young.

Who was the sculptor?
This heroic figure, resplendent in eternal youth, is the work of a Greek sculptor Cleomenes the Athenian, who inspired himself on a particular model of heroes invented in Greece in the 5th century BC by Polykleitus of Argos.

Is this a portrait?
Yes, as a portrait of Marcellus it is realistic, but the body is ideal. The tortoise at the man's foot symbolises Venus, from whom the whole dynasty claimed to be descended.

▶ *Funerary Portrait of Marcellus, nephew and son-in-law of Augustus, ca. 20 BC. Greek marble. H. 1.8 m.*

The rise and fall of the Roman Empire

The life of Roman emperors was not all play, by any means. They commanded a huge empire that stretched from Britain in the west to the Indus in southern Asia; they also had to maintain civil rest in Rome. The history of some emperors is a succession of tragedies, assassinations, incest, and coups d'état, interspersed with further conquests and civilising missions.

Delusions of grandeur

This is the face of an anxious young man, as his expression well demonstrates. The marks in the marble around his chin indicate early growth of a beard.

◀ *Emperor Caligula,* ca. 40 AD. Marble. H. 47 cm.

Who is this young emperor?
He is Caligula, son of Germanicus and Agrippina, and grandson of Antony, the grandnephew and adoptive son of Tiberius. Caligula took over from Augustus and became the third emperor in 37 AD at the age of 25. His reign was a prime example of despotism in its worst excesses, and his name has become synonymous with pride, cruelty, greed, and madness. Caligula was murdered, and although his successors Claudius and Nero did nothing to improve the reputation of Roman emperors, they did expand the Empire, however.

Hadrian, the emperor who became a god

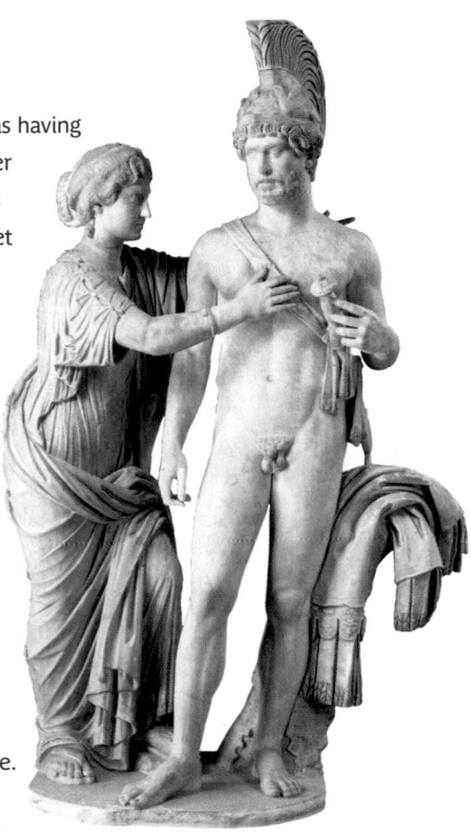

The emperor Hadrian is depicted here as having a full, bearded face, consistent with other portraits of him (see those opposite this statue). He is wearing a feathered helmet decorated with winged griffins. Slung over his shoulder is a short sword in a sheath decorated with palmettes; his mantle is draped over a tree-stump. The emperor here is represented as Mars, the god of war, receiving weapons from the goddess Venus.

Why is he naked?

As with the portrait of Marcellus (p. 71), nudity brings a heroic dimension to the character; the face however is a faithful portrait. Hadrian was the first emperor to be represented as a god in his lifetime.

▶ *Hadrian and Sabina as Mars and Venus,* between 120 and 140 AD. Marble. H. 1.73 m.

What was his achievement?

One of the greatest of Rome's emperors, Hadrian ruled during the 2nd century AD, when the Empire was at the peak of its splendour. He brought the era of conquests to a close and surrounded the Empire in a defensive frontier against the "barbarians". Hadrian was a man of letters, and passionate about the arts. He travelled the length and breadth of his dominions, founding new towns and restoring monuments. It was also Hadrian who made it unlawful for masters to kill their slaves, or they risked imprisonment.

KID'S CORNER
Opposite the Hadrian statue, behind the Sarcophagus of the Muses, take a look at the beautiful sacrifice relief, with its expressive faces and a superb depiction of the architecture of the temple in Rome.

From the Greek pantheon to Christianity

The Latins, like the Etruscans, first adopted, then adapted the Greek religion and renamed its pantheon of gods and heroes: Zeus became Jupiter, Poseidon became Neptune, Heracles became Hercules, and so forth. But the empire itself was a mosaic of diverse religions tolerated by Rome, until the Christian religion became official.

▲ *Sarcophagus: "The Lion Hunt"*, early 3rd century. Marble. W. 2.28 m.

The myth of the African lion hunt

This relief reads like a strip cartoon, from left to right: the preparation for the hunt, the impatience of the dog ❶, the horse champing at the bit ❷, a character in a helmet ❸, (his body twisted into a spiral adds even more movement to the action). Then there is the horseback rider ❹, his face highly expressive, escorted by his dogs, aiming his spear at the lion ❺. The lion appears again down below, lying slain on the ground. The numerous hunting party is richly described in high relief, while the background full of bas-reliefs lends depth to the scene.

What does the hunt symbolise?

The scene is a depiction of the mythical hunts of the Roman religion. The lion was considered the most ferocious adversary of the mythological hero, like the Nemean lion that confronted Hercules. The lion is also symbolic of North Africa, one of Rome's main colonies.

▲ *City Gate Sarcophagus,* late 4th century. Marble. W. 2.52 m.

Christian Rome

In the centre, Christ ① is shown standing on a rock within an elaborate niche, delivering a scroll containing the new divine law to Saint Peter ② , on his left; Saint Paul ③ and the other apostles are to his right. The scene takes place against a background of crenellated city walls.

How did the Empire become Christian?

It was Constantine I, who ruled from 306 to 337, who made the triumph of Christianity possible in the Empire. Christian sarcophagi discovered in Gaul can be found in the next room.

Where does this sarcophagus come from?

It was found in Rome, under the first basilica of Saint Peter in the Vatican, which became the centre of Christianity, when this was adopted as the empire's official religion after the death of Constantine I in 337.

Daily life and the art of living

The Roman living environment shows a high degree of refinement, and the sumptuous villas of the aristocracy were decorated with the finest murals and mosaics. The funerary monuments of the upper classes also reveal this refinement, and tell us much about the daily lives of Roman citizens, in particular how their children were educated. Furthermore, skilled craftsmen of all kinds produced an astounding range of furniture and ceremonial tableware, sophisticated utensils, and exquisite jewellery.

The education of young Romans

Scenes of children playing ball is a familiar theme in Roman art, but the tone is far removed from historic reliefs and sarcophagi. Here, on the left a young boy is depicted throwing a ball at a tilted board. Another child, flanked by two team-mates, one with his arm raised, is shown receiving the ball. Ovid, in *The Walnut Tree* (67-86), tells of a similar game played with walnuts, also using a tilted board. On the right, there are three young girls jumping and juggling with balls.

▶ *Bas-relief fragment, children playing ball,* 2nd quarter of the 2nd century. Marble. 22.5 x 69 cm.

Are children often represented?

Children were frequent subjects for Roman art, especially in funerary art. Children who died young were buried in a tomb and mourned just as they are today. Moments from their brief existence were depicted on the tomb, as well as images of what their afterlife would be like; the small child Hercules displayed on the same podium is an example of this.

What was their education like?

Only the richest Romans received a full education. On the other side of the podium, there is a relief showing children competing in Olympic sports, illustrating the famous motto: *"Mens sana in corpore sano"* ("A healthy mind in a healthy body"), another heritage of Greek culture.

Refinement at home

This mosaic, composed of hundreds of tiny pieces of marble and limestone, looks very much like an oriental rug. It depicts a bed of roses, surrounded by ibexes, with the legendary phoenix, symbol of immortality, at its centre.

◀ *Floor mosaic of a phoenix with roses* (close-up on the phoenix), late 5th century. Marble and limestone. 6 x 4.25 m.

Where were mosaics to be found?

Most were found in the remains of rich Roman houses, but they were also used to decorate buildings like public baths and thermae, or hot-water fountains. Mosaics typically illustrated the refinement of Roman architecture and settings.

How was a mosaic made?

A drawing was made on the ground, then the craftsman arranged coloured squares and set them with cement to obtain a smooth, solid surface, which was easy to maintain. While mosaics were already used by the Greeks, it was the Romans who really developed the mosaic, using stone, glass or terracotta to make them.

▶▶ *Go up the staircase featuring the Winged* Victory of Samothrace *to the first floor, and walk through Room 34 displaying Antique glassware to reach Room 33.*

The treasure beneath the ash

When Vesuvius erupted in AD 79, several cities including Pompeii and Herculaneum were buried under a thick mantle of volcanic ash. In the eighteenth century archaeologists uncovered their treasures beneath still intact. In Boscoreale, near Pompeii, a magnificent treasure-trove of silverware was discovered (displayed in Room 33), which provides a good introduction to the Salle des Bronzes (Room 34), where metalwork from the Greek and Roman civilisations is displayed.

▶ *Cup with skeletons,* late 1st century BC to early 1st century AD. Silver. H. 10.4 cm.

PRACTICAL INFO
From the Pyramid, head to the Richelieu wing; on the lower ground floor take the large escalator to the first floor and the treasures of the Decorative Arts collection. Next, head back to the ground floor, where you will find the Sculpture collections around the Cour Marly.

The Middle Ages is the name generally applied to the period of European history between the fall of the Roman Empire and the humanist Renaissance in Italy. For a long time considered obscure and "barbarian", today this period has been extensively rediscovered in all its wealth. The age saw the spread of Christianity throughout Europe, but also the birth and development of Islam; it was thus a period of great creativity, producing much original religious art, first in the "Romanesque" style then in the "Gothic" style. The political and social dimension of the age is also important, as we shall see in the representations of princes, knights, prelates, burghers, and peasants, who made up medieval society.

CHRONOLOGY (MAIN DATES)

476: fall of the western Roman Empire, the "barbarian" invasion
496: conversion of the French king, Clovis I, to Christianity
622: Hijra, the inception of the Muslim calendar
800: Charlemagne is crowned emperor in Rome, and Aix-la-Chapelle appointed capital
987: start of the Capetian dynasty in France (which continued to 1789)
1099: capture of Jerusalem, First Crusade
1453: the Turks take Constantinople
1455: first book printed by Gutenberg in Mayence (Germany)
1492: discovery of America

THE FALL OF THE ROMAN EMPIRE

The Emperor Triumphant. **Panel of an ivory diptych. Room 1.**
At the centre of the composition is one of the great emperors of the eastern Roman Empire, Justinian (483-565). Above him, the presence of Christ is a reminder that the Christian religion was by now the official form of worship. On the right, is a winged Victory in the Antique tradition. In the lower part of the diptych are "barbarians" paying homage to their vanquisher. Justinian was the last to resist the break-up of the Roman Empire. During his reign, he re-conquered Italy and North Africa from the Ostrogoths and Vandals, and secured peace with the Persians. He also built the basilica of Saint Sophia in the capital of Constantinople.

Rediscovering
the Middle Ages

The birth of Europe

In the late 8th century, calm returned to the turmoil of Europe thanks to the policies of the exceptional French prince, Charlemagne (742-814). After his death, the empire was divided up, and the area that would later become France was taken by his grandson Charles II the Bald (823-877). After Charlemagne, the new kingdoms became bitter rivals. In the kingdom of France, the Île-de-France and Paris played an important role, as well as the basilica of Saint-Denis, the site of a royal mausoleum and fabulous treasure-trove.

In the Antique tradition

This statue looks very similar to that of a Roman emperor on horseback, but it is in fact either Charlemagne or Charles the Bald. Although small, this bronze statuette has monumental qualities. The Emperor was the ruler of the whole of Europe; he was first king of the Francs and Lombards, then emperor of the west. Here he is depicted bearing all the symbols of his power: the orb and sceptre (the sceptre has disappeared). The horse is possibly an Antique sculpture that has been recycled.

▸ *Equestrian statuette of Charlemagne* or *Charles the Bald,* 9th century. Bronze with traces of gilding. H. 25 cm.

How did Charlemagne become emperor?

Charlemagne was the grandson of Charles Martel, the founder of the Carolingian dynasty and son of Pippin the Short. He set out to conquer a vast territory from the Atlantic to the Adriatic and from the Baltic to the Mediterranean. He was crowned emperor at Christmas AD 800 by Pope Leo III and established his capital at Aix-la-Chapelle in the centre of Europe, of which he is the "founding father". During his reign, there is said to have been a "renaissance" in the arts, but also in writing, with the adoption of the Carolingian miniscule script that is still used today.

The treasure of the Abbey of Saint-Denis

A vase of hard, red porphyry was transformed into an eagle with a head, claws and wings of silver-gilt. The eagle was symbolic of royal power in Mesopotamia, or divine power for Zeus in Greece. Here, it represents the power of the Christian religion in the Capetian kingdom.

▲ *Porphyry vase: "Suger's Eagle" vase: Egypt or Imperial Rome, mount: Saint-Denis, before 1147. Red porphyry, silver-gilt, niello.*

Where does the vase come from?

The vase dates from Antiquity and was crafted in imperial Rome. Porphyry is a hard stone which was supplied by Egypt; emperors particularly liked its red hue. The vase was part of the treasure of the royal abbey of Saint-Denis, where the *regalia*, the "crown jewels" used for the coronation of kings, were conserved. Abbé Suger transformed the vase into an eagle in the 12th century to enhance the object's value.

▸▸Return to the ground floor; at the end of the chain of galleries, in Room 5, take the library staircase to the Cour Marly, and go through to Room 1 of the Sculpture department.

KID'S CORNER

Children love the *regalia*, the French crown jewels: sword, crown, sceptre, and the rest of the royal panoply. Do not miss the *Serpentine paten* (Case 3), which again was cast in Antiquity and transformed later into a religious treasure.

Roman architecture

Just as the texts of the Christian religion originate in the Bible, telling the ancient history of the Near East, Roman builders inherited the architecture of Graeco-Roman Antiquity, features of which they perpetuated, such as round-arched stone vaults. The arches were supported by columns crowned with capitals. Western sculptors freely interpreted the classical decorative repertoire and would trim Antique features to make them match the tastes of the day.

Roman art, the heir of Antiquity

A church door in the Louvre?
There is a long tradition of leaving architecture in its original place, circumstances permitting, so this is rare example of imported architecture at the Louvre. The chapel in Saint Gilles, a former Greek settlement in the southern Gard region, is still standing.

▲ *Doorway decorated with a pattern of foliage, birds, palm leaves and interlacing,* priory of Saint Cécile d'Estagel (Gard), first quarter of the 12th century. Sandstone and limestone.

Why the naive sculpture?
We can see the naivety of the stonecutter's art in the rendering of the animals in the decor, and the capitals of the columns, which are a clumsy imitation of the Roman Corinthian order. By this time, artisans did not have the finest models of Antiquity at hand to imitate, or the same aesthetic aims.
They perpetuated the general principles of architecture with its columns and capitals, while abandoning its canons.

A diverse and decorative repertoire

This character crouching uncomfortably, head on hand, does not seem in the least bit frightened by the two lions at his side. It must be said the feline pair do not seem too ferocious. Unlike many limestone capitals, this one is sculpted in marble, a noble material that is much more difficult to work.

▲ *Daniel in the lion's den*, capital from the ancient abbey of Sainte-Geneviève-de-Paris, 6th and early 12th century. Marble. 49 x 53 cm.

Why the use of marble?

This capital was re-sculpted from another, older capital taken from a Merovingian basilica. The original was decorated with acanthus leaves, a distinctive motif of the Corinthian style. The capital no doubt came from a prestigious building because marble was costly to import.

Who is Daniel?

Daniel is the hero of an episode in the Ancient Testament, from the Book of Daniel. He was a Jewish captive under the reign of Nebuchadnezzar II, and became a close advisor to the king. He was thrown, however, into the lion's den for worshiping his own god, but the lions did not want to eat him. Daniel is also known for his prophecies, which were taken to heart by all manner of people, including Alexander the Great, since Daniel prophesised the fall of Persia to Greek hands.

83

In the fields and in the city

Medieval society was clearly compartmentalised. At its summit was the king, surrounded by his family and senior nobility, who controlled a still modest administration. The countryside was ruled by many powerful monasteries and the nobility, who controlled the peasantry. Cities, meanwhile, were hubs of trade, and tried to retain independence from the crown.

Roll out the barrel!

This capital was re-sculpted into an older floral motif and, in its place, the sculptor recounted a story in two episodes. On the left **1**, a winegrower heavily laden with freshly picked grapes makes to empty them into a vat and, in the same movement, climb into the vat to press them with his feet. On the right **2**, another grower is pouring the precious nectar obtained into a barrel.

Did you say "feet"?
The technique of treading grapes for wine is not often used today, but it was common from early Antiquity. It was only later that monks in the Burgundy region of France invented more effective and less messy grape-pressing methods.

What were the other agricultural activities of the 12th century?
As in the past, cereals dominated, because bread was the basic foodstuff. Farmers harvested other crops such as fruit and vegetables and raised cattle, under the protection of the all-powerful feudal seigneurs, and in exchange for their servitude.

▲ *Grape harvesting*, **capital from the Benedictine church of Moutiers-Saint-Jean (Burgundy region), ca. 1125. Stone. 63 x 63 cm.**

Underneath the ramparts...

This is a section of a large retable from an outhouse of the royal abbey of Saint-Denis, illustrating three scenes from the New Testament.
The symbolic representation of a city with clusters of buildings within fortifications recalls Roman sarcophagi (see p. 75).

▸ *The Annunciation, the glorious Madonna and the baptism of Christ*, retable from the church at Carrières-sur-Seine (section), late 12th century. Limestone, polychrome traces. 90 x 184 cm.

Were there cities in the 12th century?
In this period there was an "urban renaissance". With flourishing trade and greater security, new metropolises sprung up around Europe, like Bourges, Bruges and Venice. Protected behind walls, they were often independent from the feudal seigneurs. Within their walls the bourgeoisie was born and conditions were ripe for the development of the arts and culture.

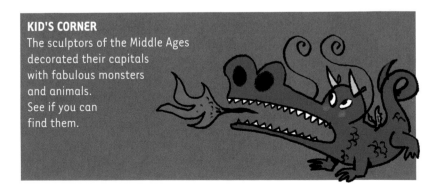

KID'S CORNER
The sculptors of the Middle Ages decorated their capitals with fabulous monsters and animals.
See if you can find them.

The Gothic revolution

Abbé Suger was the instigator of a new style of building, known as Gothic architecture. The French borrowed the "ogive" diagonal ribs (such as on Notre-Dame) from the English and, in the Île-de-France, went on to build some of the most beautiful cathedrals. Founded on the belief that God is light, Gothic churches became lighter, and daringly higher, rising up into the sky to allow the sun's rays to pour through their sumptuous stained-glass windows. The refinement of their sculpture made this era a high point of art in France.

Refinement

Room 4 contains a great number of sculptures dating from the 13th century in the Île-de-France, which are striking for their quality. This fragment of rood screen, from Chartres Cathedral, illustrates the meticulous work of those who transcribed writing and illuminations in handwritten books, before the invention of writing. Here Matthew is depicted seated beneath broken Gothic arches.

▲ *An angel dictating to the evangelist Saint Matthew,* fragment of the rood screen of Chartres Cathedral, late 13th century. Limestone. 64 x 50 cm.

Who were the "scribes" of the Middle Ages?

Originally the role was almost exclusive to monks in their monasteries, who were responsible for transcribing holy works. But as cities and the State developed, a number of laymen also learned how to write.

Was this a new form of architecture?

Completely. Roman architecture used semicircular arches, whereas Gothic architecture is distinguished by pointed arches and ribbed vaults. Chartres has one of the most beautiful Gothic cathedrals. A rood screen is an ornamented altar screen that separates the choir of the church from the nave.

The gentleness of a face

This statue is remarkable for the quality of its sculpture and the gentleness and calm of its face, which resembles that of the angels surrounding it, some of which are smiling. The movement of the beard and hair and the lighter hang of the gown are signs of a return to more balanced forms, far removed from Romanesque naivety.

Who was Childebert?

Childebert was a Merovingian king (497-558), and son of Clovis, who made Paris his capital. From a war in Spain he brought back the precious relics of Saint Vincent, and founded the abbey of Saint-Germain-des-Prés to house them. This commemorative statue was placed in the refectory of the abbey.

▸ *King Childebert, founder of the abbey of Saint-Germain-des-Prés in Paris*, 1239-44. Limestone, polychrome traces. 1.91 x 0.53 m.

KID'S CORNER
• Pay a visit to Room 6, where the Madonna and Child provides a marvellous illustration of the delicate refinement of 14th-century Gothic art.
• In Room 8, look out for a mysterious face hidden in foliage, like some fantastic metamorphosis has taken place.

The late Middle Ages

From the late 14th century in Italy and late 15th century in France, artists started taking a new direction. They now adhered to the humanist Renaissance, which turned its back on the Middle Ages and advocated a return to the rules of Classicism from Antiquity. Forms deemed "barbarian" were abandoned for models originating in Rome or Florence. At the same time, the European horizon expanded with the discovery of America.

The end of feudal chivalry

The realism and power of this funerary monument have not waned over time. The deceased knight is lying on a slab born by eight mourners, each representing a line of noble descent with their coats of arms.

▲ *Tomb of Philippe Pot (1428-1493),*
Grand Senechal of Burgundy, late 15th century.
Polychrome stone. 1.81 x 2.60 x 1.67 m.

Who was the knight?

Philippe Pot was one of the most important knights of his time; he was Seigneur de la Roche, a well-connected diplomat, and advisor to the Duke of Burgundy before King Louis XI made him the governor of the region, which was a part of the French kingdom. These were not his only titles: he was also Chevalier of the Golden Fleece, chief chamberlain, chief advisor to the king, Chevalier of the Order of Saint Michael and governor to the dauphin, the future Charles VIII. He was a great orator, and his nickname was "Mouth of Cicero". He is responsible for the almost democratic notion of "national sovereignty", a notion of power outstripping the power of princes.

Italy, the battlefield and source of inspiration

A fight to the death opposes a dragon and a horseman armed with a lance, whose battledress looks more Roman than Medieval and chivalrous. A young lady, apparently lost in the landscape, looks on fearfully.

◄ Michel Colombe (ca. 1430 to 1512/15), *Saint George and the Dragon*. Marble. 1.28 x 1.82 m.

What is the scene about?

It is an allegory of the victory of faith in God over the demon. The story of Saint George was made popular by the crusades. George was a martyred Greek Christian from the 3rd century. It is said he freed a town from a dragon that was terrorising it, and saved the king's daughter, who was next to be devoured. This relief once decorated the chapel of the Château de Gaillon, which belonged to Cardinal Georges d'Amboise. George D'Amboise was prime minister to King Louis XII in 1498, and took part in the war against Italy. He dreamed of becoming pope, and was one of the first patrons of Renaissance art in France.

This is one of the first artists actually named for his work.

From the Renaissance onwards, artists developed an important social status and laid claim to the authorship of their works. Michel Colombe famous even in his day, and one of the first, along with Italian sculptors, to adopt the ideas of the Renaissance and create his works in Carrara marble.

The panorama of the Middle Ages we provide is focused largely on France. You can expand your horizons in the Italian and North European sculpture room (Denon, lower ground floor, Donatello Gallery, Rooms 1 and 3, Rooms A, B, and C), but also in the first rooms of the Decorative Arts (Richelieu, first floor), or in the rooms devoted to Islamic art.

PRACTICAL INFO
From the Pyramid, head towards the Denon wing, go up to the ground floor passing through the Salle du Manège, where you can take in the animal decor. Cross the Daru Gallery, a veritable compendium of Antique models for humanist Europe, then climb the staircase of the Winged Victory of Samothrace, and turn right to enter the entrance hall of the Napoleon Museum, the decor of which was designed by two great Empire architects: Percier and Fontaine.

The Renaissance heralded an authentic revolution of ideas and forms, whose introduction sounded the death knell of the Middle Ages, its political organisation, philosophy, and the "Gothic" style, now deemed "barbaric". The Renaissance marked a return to the classical aesthetics of Antiquity, the heritage of which had lived on in philosophical and literary texts. The underlying humanism of the Renaissance challenged the Christian religion, and provoked opposition between Catholics and Protestant reformers. Born in the late 14th century, this movement won over France and Europe throughout the 15th and 16th centuries.

THE RETURN TO ANTIQUITY AS THE IDEAL
Alessandro Filipepi, known as Botticelli (1445-1510), *Venus and the Three Graces Presenting Gifts to a Young Woman*, fresco, ca. 1483-85. 2.11 x 2.83 m. *A Young Man is Greeted by the Liberal Arts*, fresco, ca. 1483-85. 2.37 x 2.69 m. Room 1.

These two frescoes from a villa in the outskirts of Florence represent Venus introducing a young woman to the three Graces, and a young man to seven women representing the liberal arts. Modern costumes are combined with the kind of drapery found on Roman statues, which were enjoying a period of rediscovery. The works were painted to celebrate the marriage of a young couple in Florence, the heartland of the first Renaissance. The man is shown receiving the arts and sciences, while the woman receives feminine grace; both are gifts from the goddess of love, the mistress of arts and knowledge. This heritage of Antique culture is indeed an allegory, and a paragon of humanist tastes.

From the Renaissance to the birth of the Modern: Europe goes Italian

Antique vs. Gothic

In the late 14th century, Florence adhered to the new ideas propagated by the scholarly and erudite. Brunelleschi built the dome of the city's cathedral, started by Giotto, and invented the principles of central perspective, which also provided a new vision of the world.

Tuscany, cradle of the arts in the late Middle Ages

This altarpiece once belonged in the church of San Francesco in Pisa, the Tuscan city known for its leaning tower. The piece depicts the life of Saint Francis (1182-1226), who came from Assisi in neighbouring Umbria. In the upper panel, we see him receiving the stigmata of Christ; the lower panel contains three small scenes, including Saint Francis preaching to the birds.

Why does the saint talk to birds?
Francis of Assisi was the son of a rich merchant who dreamed one day of becoming a knight, so he took a vow of poverty. He is the founder of the Franciscan order and also responsible for Christmas nativity scenes. According to legend, he made a sermon to the birds starting with the words: "My brothers, birds, you should praise your Creator very much and always love him; he gave you feathers to clothe you, wings so that you can fly, and whatever else was necessary for you."

◄ ▲ Giotto di Bondone (ca. 1265-1337),
Saint Francis of Assisi Receiving the Stigmata, ca. 1295-1300.
3.13 x 1.63 m.

The rivalry between cities

This fantastic battle set against a black background involves a large number
of soldiers, horsemen, and infantrymen, whose legs and lances form a very
complex pattern. At the centre, one particular cavalier bears a resemblance
to the portraits of Roman emperors on horseback.

▲ Paolo di Dono, known as Uccello (1397-1475), *The Battle of San Romano*,
ca. 1435-1440. 1.82 x 3.17 m.

How did Paolo Uccello avoid chaos?
He made use of a new rigorous scientific drawing method known as
"perspective". The legs of the horses, and those of the soldiers in different
colours, create the illusion of depth, as does the ground, which appears
chequered like a draughts board.

KID'S CORNER
Take a sharp right turn
into the Salle des Sept Mètres
to look at Sassetta's amusing
paintings, with a monk
"flying like a rocket" and
a magical princess painted
by Pisanello.

Did the battle really take place?
Yes. Florence waged war against the forces
of Sienna and won on 1 June 1432. The
painting belongs to a series of three that
Laurenzo de' Medici, the great prince and
patron of the Renaissance, hung in this
bedroom. The two others are in London
and Florence.

▶▶ *The Salon Carré once housed the annual exhibition of the Académie Royale de
Peinture, and gave its name to all other "salons", such as the annual car salon presenting
new automobiles. It opens onto the spectacular Grand Gallery, exhibiting
the masterpieces of the Italian Renaissance.*

The human condition

The 15th century, referred to as the Quattrocento (1400s) in Italy, was one of maturity for an art that resumed the canons of ancient Classicism, and thereby abandoned the naivety of the medieval universe for good. While religious subjects still predominated, the artists also produced lively sensitive portraits for their contemporaries.

▲ Andrea Mantegna (1431-1506) *Crucifixion*, 1456-59. 76 x 96 cm.

Excelling the classical canons of beauty

The traditional scene of the suffering of Jesus on the Cross is treated here with archaeological care. The scene of Roman soldiers dressed in the style of the period, recounts an episode that is both sacred and historic. The rigorous construction and perspective contrast with the liberties the painter took with the landscape.

Is there not a contradiction between Humanism and the Christian faith?

In one sense, yes, but as in this painting, the suffering of Christ is depicted as the suffering of the individual as he confronts the hardships of his life on Earth, all the while hoping for eternal life.

In this sense, man is seen as a divine creation, the image of God. This merging of religions, similar to the Egyptians, was only questioned later in the Enlightenment.

The ages of life

This double portrait, that of a Florentine man and his grandson, perfectly expresses the humanism of the Renaissance. The painter obeys the constraints of realism, to the point of depicting the skin disease on the man's nose, and gives us an allegorical vision of love.

Who is the painter?
Ghirlandaio was the son of a silversmith, and was widely sought-after as a portrait artist by the Florentine aristocracy. He worked with Botticelli and even counted Michelangelo among his pupils.

▸ Domenico Ghirlandaio (1449-94) *Old Man and a Child*, ca. 1490. 62 x 46 cm.

Are there not two paintings in one?
The landscape seen through the open window is an outstanding work in its own right. Landscapes as such were not yet considered worthy as a subject, which is why this one appears in the background, and yet it receives the same delicate treatment, as do the landscapes in the paintings of Leonardo da Vinci.

A pantheon of Artists

The 16th century saw a second major revolution in ideas, the Reform. The Reform was a movement led by Luther and Calvin, which contested the power of the Roman Catholic Church. The result was the conversion of northern Europe to Protestantism. It also gave rise to a Counter-Reform in Rome. The Church demanded of art that it become more militant and religious, and ordered spectacular architectural or pictorial works. The greatest artists of the time, Leonardo da Vinci, Michelangelo or Raphael, dominated a movement of committed artists which spread throughout Europe.

▶ Leonardo di ser Piero da Vinci, known as Leonardo da Vinci (1452-1519), *The Virgin of the Rocks* (1483-99). Oil on wood, transposed to canvas in 1806. 1.99 x 1.22 m.

That famous smile...

The *Mona Lisa* (see p. 11) is not the only painting by Leonardo da Vinci, it is simply the one people know best. In the *Virgin of the Rocks*, the landscape seems to be an essential part of the composition. The Madonna rescues the young Saint John the Baptist, an orphan abandoned in a cave, under the protection of the archangel Uriel, kneeling on his right. The faces express the same gentleness, and wear the same smile as the Mona Lisa. But here the cave adds a dramatic dimension, which seems to foretell the destinies of the young children. Note too the marvellous interplay of the figures' hands on the canvas.

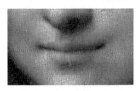
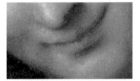
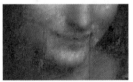

▸ **Leonardo di ser Piero da Vinci, known as Leonardo da Vinci (1452-1519),** *The Virgin of the Rocks; Mona Lisa; Saint John the Baptist; The Virgin and Child with Saint Anne* **(detail).**

What is the story behind this work?

It was one of the most beautiful paintings in François I's collection. Unfinished when Leonardo left Milan in 1499, it was bought by the king, along with the *Mona Lisa*, when the painter came to live in France in 1516. According to legend, Leonardo died in the arms of the doting king himself.

Why did Leonardo come to France?

At the end of his life, after a long career as a painter, architect, engineer, scholar, inventor, theoretician of the arts, humanist philosopher, and astute strategist, Da Vinci, the universal man, must have looked forward to a peaceful retirement. The opportunity for this was provided by the French king, François I, who also hoped to take advantage of his multiple talents in both civil and military areas. And take advantage he did; Leonardo was asked to design the Château de Chambord.

▲ Raffaello Santi, known as Raphael
(1483-1520). *Self-portrait with a friend*,
ca. 1518/19. 99 x 83 cm.

Artists as powerful as princes

This superb double portrait does not depict princes or saints, but two artists, and was painted by one of the most famous, Raphael, who is here on the left. The simplicity of their clothes shows certain modesty. Look at Raphael's gaze, as well as the movement of the hand in front and the finger directed at the viewer, which seem to surge from the canvas.

What was the social position of an artist like Raphael?
One of the highest possible at the time. He was Pope Julius II's own appointed painter and architect, like Michelangelo. Raphael's loggia at the Vatican sits side-by-side Michelangelo's Sistine Chapel. We are far removed from the small provincial workshops where daubers were rife. Official artists were respected and celebrated in their lifetime.

Who is the friend with whom Raphael has chosen to associate his image for posterity?
It could be the painter Pordenone or Pontormo, Giulio Romano or Antonio da Sangallo, whose works are also exhibited in the Grand Gallery. It might also be Pietro Aretino, a witty writer and dramatist whom Raphael had met in Rome. A friend of Titian, he lived out his days in Venice and is said to have died from a fit of laughter.

▶▶ *On the right of the Grand Gallery is a large room devoted to 16th-century Venetian painting, dominated by Titian, Tintoretto, and Veronese with his famous painting,* The **Wedding Feast at Cana**. *The room also houses the most famous painting in the world, the* **Mona Lisa** *(Rooms 6 and 7; see p. 11).*

The decor of Venice, the "Soronissimo"

Veronese's *The Wedding Feast at Cana* covers nearly 70 square metres and is the largest conserved in a French museum. It contains no fewer than 132 characters, and originally decorated the Benedictine refectory of San Giorgio Maggiore in Venice. Beneath a marvellous blue sky, surrounded by classicising architecture, the only figures who look out at the observer are Christ at the centre, and the bride on the left.

▲ Paolo Caliari, known as Veronese (1528-88), *The Wedding Feast at Cana* (1563). 6.77 x 9.94 m.

How did this huge work end up at the Louvre?

It was Bonaparte's armies who brought the painting back to Paris and it was first hung in the Louvre in 1798. When works requisitioned in Italy were returned after the Empire, the Restoration monarchy used the painting's size as an excuse to retain it.

What architecture! And what a celebration!

Veronese made a name for himself in Venice for his spectacular decorative painting. Here he offers us the image of a huge celebration, where the guests, dressed in Renaissance styles and not those of Antiquity, cavort in a setting inspired by Andrea Palladio, the famous architect of San Giorgio Maggiore.

Mannerism and phantasmagoria

In the second half of the 16th century, when Renaissance art had reached what is considered its pinnacle, various new artistic currents began to emerge, offering new directions. Works with religious or profane themes were less dependent on the demands of the state, and started expressing greater freedom. Some adopted a "manner", which spread through a Europe that was already won over by the Italian spirit.

▲ Jacopo Carrucci, known as Pontormo (1494-1556), *Madonna and Child with Saint Anne and Four Saints*, ca. 1527-29. Panel (poplar). 2.28 x 1.76 m.

Indolent forms

Forms became unusually elongated, movement became more complex and forced, while colours became more lively and contrasted. This was a far cry from the sublime poise of Raphael. Artists also strove to give more expression to even conventional subjects. Here, for example, the dynamic composition makes the child appear to writhe to free himself, while his mother restrains him with infinite gentleness.

What is Mannerism?

Mannerism comes from the Italian word *maniera*, and refers to a style of painting from the 1530s. The sack of Rome by Charles V in 1527 rattled humanist convictions, and the mood across Europe became tense. That tension brought changes to art and architecture, with the Baroque style, which expressed much more freedom and imagination, breaking free of the strict rules of the early Renaissance. One of Raphael's pupils, Giulio Romano, was an important exponent of these changes, and his work greatly influenced the Fontainebleau School in France (see p. 108).

Why was this *Madonna and Child* painted?

It was a commission by the Florentine government to commemorate the expulsion of a medieval tyrant. But it was also painted shortly before Emperor Charles V's troops laid siege to the city in 1529. Saint Anne is the patron saint of Florence, whereas Saint Sebastian, Saint Benedict, and the penitent thief holding the Cross, are the patron saints of a "happy death" along with Saint Michael.

▲ Giuseppe Arcimboldo (1527-93),
The Four Seasons, 1573. 76 x 63 cm (each).

An original artist

This work offers a marvellous optical illusion. Approach the canvas and the faces disappear leaving only their "ingredients" - fruit, vegetables, and mushrooms, which symbolise the seasons. The work is a celebration of the abundance and generosity of nature, and also shows a great sense of humour and imagination.

Idealism vs. realism

In the late 16th century, new possibilities opened up. On the one hand, the Classicism of the Carracci brothers hailed the arrival of Academicism, while Caravaggio's realism announced the arrival of anti-establishment movements in painting.

The Classical rule

The swirling composition opposes and separates the celestial world, where the Madonna seems to float in a golden light on a cloud of zephyrs and cherubs, from the terrestrial world, where the evangelist appears enraptured. There is also an apparently abandoned artist's palette on the ground.

▸ **Annibale Carracci (1560-1609),** *The Virgin Appearing to Saint Luke and Saint Catherine,* **1592. 4.01 x 2.26 m.**

What does it all mean?

It is believed that Luke himself, one of the founders of the Church, painted a portrait of the Madonna, an icon, whereby he is hailed as the patron saint of painters. Luke was a doctor by training, and is therefore also the patron saint of the health and legal professions. He is present twice in this work, the second time in the sky accompanied by the other evangelists, his bull, and a huge book. We can see here that verisimilitude and realism are not important for Annibale Carracci, whose Academy of Desiderosi would inspire the classicising art of the 17th and 18th centuries.

What about Saint Catherine?

Saint Catherine of Alexandria is the patron saint of barbers, cartwrights, ropemakers, drapers, school children and students, millers, solicitors, wet-nurses, orators, philosophers, plumbers, potters, preachers, knife grinders, tailors, theologians, turners, and not least unwedded women.

The freedom of the artist

A moment for silence
and contemplation. A ray of natural
light breaks through the darkness,
emphasising the sanctity of the
scene, but apart from the faint
halo, there are no symbols or
attributes to tell us of the identity
of the deceased and his entourage.
The scene seems very real; death
is portrayed with suffering
and lament.

▸ Michelangelo Merisi, known as
Caravaggio (1571-1610), *The Death of
the Virgin*, 1601-1605/06. 3.69 x 2.45 m.

How was the painting received at the time?

The work caused an outrage. The monks who had commissioned it for their
church rejected their painting, as they found it too crude. Caravaggio effectively
based his Madonna on the body of a drowned woman. Furthermore, the setting
for this highly emotional scene is provided by mere workshop drapery.
Eventually, it was Louis XIV who bought it for his collection.

What is "Caravaggism"?

This is the name used to designate the European artistic current, which
imitated, if not Caravaggio's poetic grandeur, at least his realism and his
extraordinary command of light and chiaroscuro, the technique based on
the use of light and shade.

> *If you want to see the effect that Italian Renaissance painting had on France,
> visit the Richelieu wing on the second floor. Here you will also find the works
> of Flemish, Dutch, and German artists, who were painting at the same time
> but producing very different work. Renaissance works also feature in the Italian
> Sculpture department (Denon, ground floor) and in the Decorative Arts department
> (Richelieu, first floor).*

PRACTICAL INFO

From the Pyramid, go via the Richelieu wing to the second floor and the French Painting department. Here you will first encounter the Portrait of John, Duke of Normandy, who went on to become King John II the Good from 1350 to 1364, one of the first builders of the Louvre palace. Make your way through the first rooms, then in Room 6 you will find the Portrait of Charles VII the Victorious, by Jean Fouquet, which marks the end of the Middle Ages. In the same room, take a look at Suzanne de Bourbon and the Retable of the Parliament of Paris for the view of the medieval Louvre behind Saint Louis IX (on the right is Charlemagne with his sword).

While Italy was the beacon of Renaissance Europe, from the 17th century, France took over, and Paris became the most powerful cultural capital of the States. From the affirmation of royal authority, via the unification of the kingdom and the French language, to the establishment of modern state structures, it was a time of deep changes. The Enlightenment then opened up the way to the Revolution. Artists depicted this movement of history in official court portraits and scholarly works as well as in genre painting illustrating daily life.

FRENCH KINGS: A CHRONOLOGY

1515-1547 François I	1574-1589 Henri III	1715-1774 Louis XV
1547-1559 Henri	1589-1610 Henri IV	1774-1792 Louis XVI
1559-1560 François II	1610-1643 Louis XIII	
1560-1574 Charles IX	1643-1715 Louis XIV	

THE PRINCE OF MODERN TIMES

Jean Clouet (ca. 1480-1541), *Portrait of François I, King of France (1494-1547)*, ca. 1530. Room 7.

This portrait of the benefactor prince is a staple feature of French history books. The detail and refinement of the king's stately robes and hat are remarkable. The gaze is piercing, malicious and ironic; the smile almost mocking. His delicate hands hold the pommel of a sword, the sword of the first knight of the kingdom; the sense of royalty is reinforced by the crown motifs in the background. For a king, reconciling private life and the obligations of office was not always easy, so it was essential for the monarch to put across a perfect image to win over the support of his subjects.

The French kingdom in modern times 16th to 18th centuries

French Mannerism

In the 16th century France was still very influenced by Italy, but the period saw a distinctly French culture evolve, in both political and aesthetic terms. Given that France lay at the crossroads of Europe, it also drew influences from countries further north. At the very centre of everything stood the king, supported by his vast court composed of the main aristocratic families.

Pleasure at the court

Welcome to the French court! Room 8 presents a fantastic array of royal portraits: François I, his son Henri II, Catherine de Médicis, their son Charles IX with Elisabeth of Austria, and lastly Henri III. They are accompanied by a number of courtiers and other influential people.

This scene depicts Henri III at the wedding feast held at the Louvre palace for his friend Anne de Joyeuse. The king is sitting beneath a canopy with the queen Louise de Lorraine, and the queen mother Catherine de Médicis. The dancing newlyweds will soon be joined by the happy throng.

▸ *Wedding Ball for the Duke of Joyeuse in 1581*, late 16th century. Oil on copper. 41 x 65 cm.

Who's who?

It is hard to keep track of who is who, particularly because European royal families frequently intermarried. Lorraine, Austria, and Florence, with the Medicis: the whole of Europe attended the ball. Henri III was also the king of Poland before becoming king of France. The last of the House of Valois, Henri was a refined man and a keen opponent of violence. He was murdered, however, and his reign saw the outbreak of religious wars between Catholics and Protestants.

KID'S CORNER

Find a picture frame that you particularly like, and draw it carefully. When you get back home, you can use this to frame your own family portraits.

A portrait... unveiled

Who are these two ladies in the bath? And why is one pinching the nipple of the other, who is holding a precious ring? And what of the maid in the background, apparently absorbed in her needlework, as though pretending she has seen nothing? Maybe we too are being a little too indiscreet; although, with its red velvet curtains, the scene does look somewhat like a theatre stage.

◄ Portrait of Gabrielle d'Estrées and her sister the Duchess of Villars, ca. 1594. 96 x 125 cm.

Was the painting influenced by Italy?

Completely. The anonymous painter belonged to what was known as the "Fontainebleau School", named after the royal workshop created by François I, made up of Italian artists, including Primaticcio and Rosso Fiorentino, to initiate the French in the current trends of art. The delicate hands and refined colours are perfectly in tune with Italian Mannerism (see p. 101).

Another enigma?

The work represents, on the right, the beautiful Gabrielle d'Estrées, the official mistress of Henri IV, the king of France and Navarre, with her sister. It is only natural therefore that they bathe together. The pinched nipple is an allusion to the fact that Gabrielle will soon give birth to a child, César, Duke of Vendôme, the father of whom was the king himself. The ring is no doubt a royal gift. After Gabrielle's tragic death in 1599, the king married Marie de' Medici, the life of whom is depicted by Rubens in the Medici Gallery, Room 18.

▶ The Medici Gallery (Room 18)

Louis XIII and classical France

Louis XIII, the son of Henri IV and Marie de' Medici, was born in 1601. Under his reign France imposed its power around Europe with the important territorial conquests of Béarn, Navarre, Savoy, Piedmont, and Roussillon, among others. He drove out his mother's Italian clan, and handed the control of the state to Cardinal Richelieu, the main architect of his power; a splendid portrait of the cardinal sits alongside that of the king.

A royal pose

This royal portrait is very different to that of François I. The king is not represented as a patron but as a conqueror crowned for his victory. His sumptuous armour speckled with fleurs-de-lys is the emblem of French royalty.

Why did the king lay siege to La Rochelle?

The town of La Rochelle was a Protestant bastion; Henri III had already attempted to lay siege to the town in 1573, but in vain. It was finally down to Richelieu that Louis XIII was able to defeat the town that had benefited from privileges accorded in the Edict of Nantes by Henri IV.

▲ Philippe de Champaigne (1602-74), *Louis XIII crowned by Victory (Siege of La Rochelle, 1628)*, 1635. 2.28 x 1.75 m.

▲ Nicolas Poussin (1594-1665), *Et in Arcadia Ego*,
ca. 1638-40. 85 x 121 cm.

Poetry in painting

The shepherds are reading
a Latin inscription engraved
on this isolated countryside
tombstone: *"Et in Arcadia Ego."*
As in many of Poussin's works,
the countryside plays
an important role.

What does the inscription mean?

"I too have lived in Arcadia."
It is an invitation, characteristic
of the moral and spiritual vein
of the time, to contemplate the
irreversible nature of our destiny:
death.

Where is Arcadia?

Arcadia is an isolated mountainous
region in the centre of Greece, where the
Alphaeus and Styx rivers flow; its capital
was called Megalopolis. Poets of Antiquity
depicted Arcadia as heaven on earth,
where shepherds lived in peace and
harmony with nature. Classical culture
was very attached to its references and
the history and mythology of Antiquity.
Poussin's idyllic landscapes were very
different from classically arranged gardens
such as that of Versailles, and were
the main source of inspiration for English
gardens from the late 17th century.

▶▶ *From Room 14 to our next port of call, you have to cross fifteen large rooms. On you way,
be sure to look at other works of Poussin, including the Four Seasons, but also those of
Claude Gelée, known as Claude Lorraine, who painted magnificent sunsets over the sea.*

The three orders of society

Ancien Régime society was very hierarchical. At its peak were the king and his family, along with the nobility. Next came the clergy, and in particular the regular clergy and its monasteries, which led the Counter Reformation against the Protestants. Finally there was the people, the "Third Estate", mainly peasants, who bore the brunt of taxes and tilled the land, rarely their own.

▲ Antoine and Louis Le Nain (ca. 1600/1610-1648), *The Peasant Family*, 1.13 x 1.59 m.

The misery of the lowly

There is a sense of sadness inherent in this family scene. Their frugal meal is made up of bread, wine, and a little salt. There is a single empty bowl on the table, no candle in the candlestick, and the soup-pan on the floor is empty. The barefooted children warm themselves by a meagre fire. Not even the dog and cat bring joy to the scene, the grim silence of which is only broken by the flute-player. The delicate glass of red wine is a surprising detail.

Were peasants really so poor?

They did effectively have to face up to difficult living conditions. The reign of Louis XIII was marked by a number of wars that considerably weakened the kingdom. The increase in taxes, on salt in particular, left the people in a state of drastic misery, which gave rise to peasant revolts that were severely repressed by Richelieu. The winters were harsh and famine rife, such were the daily hardships of the essentially peasant population.

The opulence of the great

What a contrast with the peasants depicted by the Le Nain brothers! Wealth abounds here in the accumulation of details: the sumptuously harnessed white horse, richly embroidered costumes, the series of young men busying themselves around the dignitary, who is shielded by parasols like an oriental nabob, and looks almost ridiculous with his smug grin. The landscape itself has disappeared, as though effaced by the splendour of this prestigious portrait.

▲ Charles Le Brun (1619-90), *Pierre Séguier, chancellor of France* (1588-1672), ca. 1655-61. 2.95 x 3.57 m.

Who is this imposing figure?

Duke of Villemor, Pierre Séguier was a chief minister to Louis XIII. He was the Keeper of the Seal under Richelieu then became Chancellor. In 1639 he led the repression of the peasant revolts against the rise in salt tax - salt was indispensable for conserving food.

He is the very image of aristocratic wealth and of the distance separating the monarchy from the people and their misery. Séguier was a great patron, particularly of the Académie Française. He was the first to support the young artist who became the head painter of Louis XIV, Charles Le Brun.

A militant clergy

A nun seated wearing the elegant simplicity of monastic robes,
in the background we can see the wealthy abbey of Port-Royal-des-Champs,
in the valley of Chevreuse, near Paris; Mother Angélique was its abbess,
and the beneficiary of its huge revenues.

▲ Philippe de Champaigne (1602-74), *Mother Angélique Arnaud,
abbess of Port Royal*, 1654. 130 x 98 cm.

What role did she play?

Born into a powerful family, Angélique Arnaud became abbess at the age
of eleven. She was a key figure of Jansenism, a Christian doctrine inspired
by Saint Augustine, which was opposed to Humanism. She turned Port Royal
into the largest Catholic intellectual centre of its time. In the words of one Paris
archbishop: "Those nuns are as pure as angels, but as proud as demons."

The Sun King

When Louis XIV the Great came to the throne,
he was intent on ensuring his divine right to absolute
power with the aid of powerful ministers. At the head
of a centralised state that he ran from the Château
de Versailles, he increased the power of France.
His 72 years on the throne made him the longest
reigning sovereign in Europe.

▲ Charles Le Brun (1619-90), *The Entry of Alexander into Babylon, or The Triumph of Alexander*, 1665. 4.50 x 7.07 m.

Emulating the greats

This series of huge canvases illustrates the heroic deeds in the life of Alexander
the Great, the great Greek conqueror of Antiquity. He finally entered Babylon after
a series of battles, illustrated in other canvases, the story of which this painting
forms the culminating point. Alexander appears in all his glory, bedecked in white
and gold, his gold chariot is drawn by two elephants, escorted by his army
transporting the booty seized from the enemy.

Why is Alexander the Great important in the middle of the 17th century?

His depiction is a pretext, characteristic of historic painting. It is not Alexander represented here but Louis XIV. The monarch identified himself with Apollo, the god of the arts whose symbol is the sun, and also Alexander, the greatest conqueror of Antiquity. Charles Le Brun, head artist and leading portraitist of the reign, was the archetypal official artist. Founder of the Académie Royale and director of the Gobelins tapestry works, he is responsible for the some of the most impressive interior decor at the Louvre and Versailles, in particular the Apollo Gallery and the Hall of Mirrors.

The absolute monarch

This is the most famous portrait of the so-called "Sun-King", aged 63; here he is represented in all his glory. Each meticulously painted detail contributes to the exaltation of the royal person: the antique setting toned down with heavy drapery, the coronation cloak covered in fleurs-de-lys, and the royal *regalia* - the crown, sceptre and sword of Charlemagne - which was conserved at the royal basilica of Saint-Denis.

▲ Hyacinthe Rigaud (1659-1743), *Louis XIV* (1638-1715), 1701. 2.77 X 1.94 m.

Who commissioned this work?

The king himself, who intended to send it to his grandson, King Philip V of Spain. But Louis was so happy with it that he kept it for himself and had a copy made for his grandson. The painting is distinctly political, serving the purposes of absolute power. It is effectively propaganda, based on the representation of symbols and ideals, as well as on highly emphatic portraiture.

KID'S CORNER
Look out of the window, on the left you will see the monograms LL, for Louis XIV. Signatures like these can be found everywhere in the architecture of the palace: H for Henri II, N for Napoleon, and even RF for the République Française (French Republic).

▸ Jean-Antoine Watteau (1684-1721), *Pierrot,* also known as *Gilles,* ca. 1718/19. 1.85 x 1.50 m.

The Italian Comedy

This dreamy Pierrot dressed in white is one of the characters of the commedia dell'arte, along with Harlequin, Pulcinella, Colombina, and Scaramouche, whom we see at Pierrot's feet. Pierrot is a naive but honest valet, who is also an absent-minded practical joker. With his pink-ribboned shoes and ill-fitting clothes, he seems surprised to pose for such an attractive portrait. He might look ridiculous, but we sense a certain humour and irony in his gaze.

Quite a change from the stern portraits so far!

Watteau was effectively the artist of fêtes galantes, painting the Regency period of the Duke of Orléans, between the death of Louis XIV in 1715 and the accession to the throne of his great-grandson Louis XV. Louis XV was born in 1710; his reign could not start until 1722, hence the Regency period. The rocaille style was then in fashion, and after an austere end to the reign, divertissement took over. This painting was the sign for the Parisian café of a former actor, Belloni. Italian theatre troupes did not often have theatres, and frequently performed in the open air.

The pleasures of Louis XV

Louis XV succeeded his great-grandfather, and his reign of sixty years was nearly as long as that of Louis XIV. At first Louis was nicknamed "the Beloved", but as his reign progressed he became more dissolute and hence less popular. The 18th century saw the Enlightenment, which ended with the Revolution and the fall of the absolute monarchy.

▲ Charles-André van Loo, known as Carle Vanloo (1705-65), *Rest during the Hunt*, 1737. 2.20 x 2.50 m.

The art of living without etiquette

This painting as well as the *Hunt Breakfast* by Jean-François de Troy decorated the dining room of the king in the royal chateau at Fontainebleau. It provides a good illustration of the difference in character between Louis XV and his great-grandfather, as well as a great change in the representation of the private life of the sovereign. Here we see him in the company of those who helped make his reputation. It is also provides an image of the carefree joy of living of high society when removed from the cumbersome etiquette of the court.

Nature and truth

This still-life is one of the Louvre's most fascinating paintings. The fish, a skate, seems to be staring at us; however it is not the skate's eyes staring at us but its gills. While the chef's away, the cat will play, but the movement of the shells seems to have disturbed our feline friend; his fur is bristling and his ears are pricked.

▲ Jean-Siméon Chardin (1699-1779), *The Skate*, ca. 1725/26. 1.14 X 1.46 m.

What is a still-life?

Chardin was very fond of painting still lifes, inanimate every day objects without human presence: flowers, victuals, kitchen utensils, post-hunting scenes. He drew his inspiration from the Dutch painters.

▲ François Boucher (1703-70), *Morning Coffee*, 1739. 81 x 65 cm. Room 40.

Lunchtime!

This painting takes us into the heart of the family life of the painter Boucher, who lived in the Louvre, along with other artists. This work gives us an idea of the interior decor tastes of the time. The family is gathered for lunch, the parents are drinking coffee, which was particularly fashionable at the time.

KID'S CORNER

What is the child sitting on the floor doing? Is the child a boy or girl? What does he/she have around his/her head?

Literature, art, and science

This is one of the most beautiful female portraits of the Louvre. It conveys the same impression of nobility as the other royal portraits encountered to this point, and the silk dress is worthy of a queen. But the rich vein of symbolism within expresses a world of intellect and culture. There are musical instruments and scores, an album of drawings, engravings, and books including Diderot and Alembert's *Encyclopaedia*. A globe meanwhile is positioned to show France.

Who was the Marquise de Pompadour?

Jeanne-Antoinette Poisson was the official mistress of King Louis XV, who gave her the title of Marquise. This woman of great intelligence symbolises the accession of the bourgeoisie into the ruling elite, at the head of the social hierarchy. For nearly twenty years, alongside the king she practically governed France, encouraging the arts and manufacturing industries. The king offered her a house in Paris, the Hôtel Evreux, which is today the Elysée palace, the headquarters of the French president.

▲ Maurice-Quentin Delatour (1704-88),
The Marquise de Pompadour.
Pastel on blue paper. 1.75 x 1.28 m.

What are pastels?

Pastels are small drawing-sticks made of a mixture of chalk, gum arabic, and coloured pigments. Delatour was a virtuoso of this particular medium. Pastels were appreciated for their transparency and the freshness of their colours, which were ideal in the art of portraiture. On the wall opposite this portrait of the marquise is a self-portrait of Delatour himself.

The philosophy of the Enlightenment

The late 18th century is marked by the thought of philosophers who questioned the certitudes of a declining civilisation. The rise of the Third Estate driven by a bourgeoisie, which had grown rich on trade, challenged the power of the aristocracy and absolute monarchy, while secularism also questioned the power of the church. Poets and painters began to turn to new themes for inspiration.

A Return to Virtue

At the centre of this composition, the arms of the newly betrothed are tenderly entwined. Behind the bride stands the mother, distraught at her daughter's departure, and the various members of the bride's family show genuine emotion, while the clerk completing the marriage certificate looks on, impassive.

▲ Jean-Baptiste Greuze (1725-1805), *The Village Bride*, Salon of 1761. Oil on canvas. 92 x 117 cm.

What does this painting mean?
It is a painting with a moral message, and a chance to stage a provincial family at an important event. This work was particularly acclaimed by Denis Diderot, an Enlightenment philosopher, inventor of a new form of theatre, the *drame bourgeois*, and coined the term "moral painting" in his praise of Greuze. The work also extols bourgeois family life, and a return to simplicity in life as well as in the arts.

▲ Jean-Honoré Fragonard (1732-1806), *The Bolt*, 1777.
Oil on canvas. 74 x 94 cm.

Newfound freedom

The painting has a diagonal composition, relating the story. The apple on the side-table at the left is the symbol of what the young man will bite into, once he has safely bolted the door.

A risqué subject, maybe?

A number of painters, including Greuze and Fragonard, show a fondness for dissolute subjects, even erotic ones. Their treatment of such scenes was skilful nonetheless, and they avoided censure. Their works expressed the desire for freedom pervading a society that was hypocritical and moralising. Fragonard's works show a lively stroke and artistry in the use of light, which put his simple genre paintings on a par with the great historical works.

The guided tour that follows continues this exploration. If you wish to discover more about France and the Ancien Régime, visit the Sculpture rooms and the Cour Puget and Cour Marly (Richelieu, ground floor), as well as the Decorative Arts department, where furniture and decorative arts of the 16th to 18th centuries are exhibited (Richelieu and Sully wings, first floor).

From the French Revolution to the Second Empire, the life of the Louvre was full of surprises, and was greatly affected by the Revolutions of 1789, 1830, 1848 and the Commune of 1871. The period saw the empire, monarchy, and republic wrestle for power, and throughout all this turmoil, the Louvre had a special place. The museum already contained an astounding and ever-growing collection; nearby was also the residence of heads of state at the Tuileries. Along with the Tuileries Palace, to which it was joined then detached, the Louvre was "the capital of the 19th century".

FRANCE, HOME TO THE ARTS

Charles-Louis Müller (1815-92), *France engraving the profile of Napoleon III onto a marble table*, Salon of 1865 (view of ceiling, Salon Denon, Room 76).

This huge salon is remarkable for the decoration of its ceiling. It pays homage to the major patron kings: Louis IX the Saint in the Middle Ages, François I in the Renaissance, Louis XIV in the 17th century, and Napoleon I during the Empire. At the centre is a profile of Napoleon III, who built the final section of the Louvre, adjoining the old "château" with the Tuileries Palace to form a vast complex, containing not only a museum, but also imperial apartments, ministries, and various administrative bodies. The Tuileries Palace was damaged by fire during the Commune in 1871, and then completely razed in 1882.

The Age
of Revolutions

The grandeur of Antiquity

Critics have often sought to oppose Neoclassicism and Romanticism, but in reality they are part of the same universe. Whether they looked to Antiquity or the present day, the artists of the late 18th and early 19th centuries were all in search of creative autonomy, questioning the rules of Classicism, and preparing for a new world. Individual values and feelings began to take primary importance.

▲ Jacques-Louis David (1748-1825), *The Oath of the Horatii*, 1784. 3.30 x 4.25 m.

Republican virtues

The three Horatii brothers were chosen by Republican Rome to confront their enemies, the three Curiatii, from the town of Alba. Here, against a sober classicising decor, they receive their weapons from their father, and pledge to vanquish or die. On the right, their mother and sister weep, fearful they will never see them again. The vigour of the men contrasts with the limp abandon of the women.

So, who wins?

Only one of the three, Publius, survives the battle, but the Republic was saved. The sister Camilla mourned the death of her lover, one of the Curiatii, and was assassinated by her brother.

What is the story behind the work?

The painting is considered the symbol of Neoclassicism, which saw a return to Antiquity. It was painted in Rome and, when it was shown in Paris, met with huge success. It was acquired for Louis XVI's collection and turned David into the most influential artist of his time. It later became a symbol of the revolution due to its "republican" subject matter, and because the artist himself was responsible for the arts under the "Reign of Terror".

The invention of feeling

The feelings this painting emanates are of terror and misfortune. Nature unleashed and the lightning forking through the sky enhance the sense of drama. A powerful figure is carrying an ailing man on his back, and clutching his wife's hand. Will he manage to save his family from impending peril? Nothing could be less sure. The withered tree seems to symbolise defeat.

Who was Girodet?

Girodet was a pupil of David, educated in the ideals of Neoclassicism, who won the privileged Prix de Rome in 1789. He soon distinguished himself from the other pupils of the master by developing a very personal vision, in a distinctly Romantic vein, like Chateaubriand, whose novel *Atala* provided the inspiration for another of Girodet's paintings in the same room, *The Tomb of Atala*.

▸ Anne-Louis Girodet (1767-1824), *The Flood*, Salons of 1806 and 1814. 4.41 x 3.41 m.

The major Romantic works of the Salle Mollien (77) are presented in the masterpieces chapter at the beginning of this guide, namely The Raft of the Medusa *by Géricault (p. 14) and* Liberty Guiding the People *by Delacroix (p.15).*

▸▸ *Next visit the main staircase featuring the* Winged Victory of Samothrace, *and pass into the series of rooms in the Charles X museum. Right at the end in Room 27, take the spiral staircase that leads to the second floor and the French Painting rooms.*

A new age

The revolutionary period put an end to the Ancien Régime, and in its struggle against archaism sought models of virtue in Antiquity: the Athens of Pericles and the Rome of the Republic. It also gave rise to a new vision of man as an individual, with his rights and duties. The education of the people became a priority, and the place of women in society was also being considered anew.

▲ Hubert Robert (1733-1808), *Grand Gallery redevelopment project*, 1796. 1.15 x 1.45 m.

A revolutionary museum

The Louvre had always been a cornerstone of French history, and remained so even during the Revolution. Here we see a curious public visiting the Grand Gallery amidst copyists busy at work; Louis XVI's plan to open the royal collections to the public finally came to fruition. Hubert Robert was guardian of the king's paintings, and the curator of the museum that opened in 1793. Robert was a painter of architecture and ruins. Here his redevelopment proposal consisted of natural overhead lighting, an idea that was subsequently executed.

What was the vocation of the museum?

At the time, a museum was more than a place for conserving artworks; above all it had a pedagogical mission. Young artists would visit to study and copy the works of the masters, as copying formed the basis of their apprenticeship; the public would also come to learn about ancient history and contemporary events from the great paintings of history. During the Revolution, the Louvre also took in the artworks confiscated from noble émigrés and from the religious orders that were suppressed during the Reign of Terror.

Woman and citizen

The artist has lent a monumental stature to this portrait of a young West Indian woman, a freed slave brought back to France by her "master". She appears alone, dignified, and almost haughty; the superbly rendered drapery leaves one breast exposed, the white of the cloth contrasting with her skin, and highlighting her youth and beauty.

◄ Marie-Guillemine Benoist (1768-1826),
Portrait of a Black Woman, Salon of 1800.
81 x 65 cm.

How unusual was this portrait of a black woman at the time?

It was very original. The Revolution and the Empire periods saw great social advances: the revolutionary government declared the Rights of Man, instituted the Civil Code that is still in force today, and in 1974 abolished slavery in the colonies. In 1902, however, Napoleon I re-introduced slavery, and it was not until the 1848 Revolution that this evil was definitively abolished.

People at the time viewed this work as a manifesto against slavery, but also for feminism, even more so because the artist is one of the rare women painters of the time, and a pupil of Jacques-Louis David.

The urban revolution

Spurred on by the first industrial revolution, France's urban populations increased astonishingly under the Empire and the Restoration, a time that saw the birth of the "city", of which Paris was one of the symbols. Many of the artists and writers of the period, such as Balzac, immortalised its historical events, but also its daily life.

▲ Martin Drölling (1789-1851), *Kitchen interior*, 1815. 65 x 80 cm.

An apartment in the city

Drölling was a pupil of David and the winner of the 1810 Prix de Rome; he was also responsible for some of the Louvre's great decorative cycles. Here he produced a distinctly intimist vision of daily life in the early 19th century. The child playing on the floor with the cat and the women busy with their needlework near an open casement looking onto a garden or avenue, bring a peaceful atmosphere to this bourgeois Parisian interior, in an age just prior to the rapid onset of modernism, and the growing commodities of running water and gas lighting.

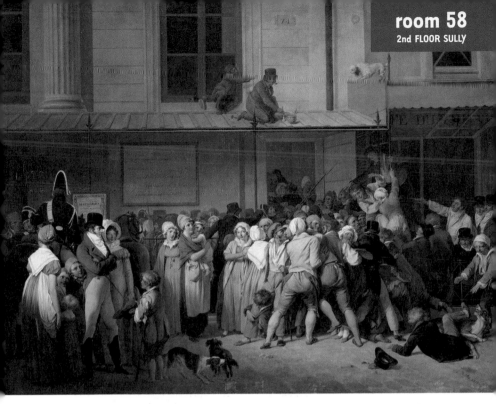

▲ Louis-Léopold Boilly (1761-1845), *The entrance to the Théâtre de l'Ambigu-Comique on the day of a free show*, 1819. 66 x 80 cm.

Passion for the theatre

Like many scenes by Boilly showing the arrival of a carriage, a bourgeois family caught in a sudden shower, a cabaret scene, or an artists' meeting, this small work provides an animated illustration of Parisian life. Paris was the capital of art, pleasure, and liberty, and attracted visitors from all over Europe. As the queue degenerates into a brawl, a bourgeois family looks on, and the constabulary prepares to intervene. Look at the wealth of detail the artist uses to bring the scene to life.

Why all this commotion?

The theatres on the central boulevards of Paris attracted huge crowds, and were very popular among the working classes. It is likely that the offer of a free performance brought a flood of people, all eager to see the show.

KID'S CORNER

Look at the painting of the family caught in a shower. The streets of Paris have changed immensely in two hundred years. Look also at how the children are dressed.

129

▲ Horace Vernet (1789-1863), *The Gate at Clichy*, 1820. 98 x 131 cm.

A return to the old order

30 March 1814: Paris was besieged by European troops allied against Napoleon I. The last focus of resistance was the city's Clichy gateway under the command of Marshal Moncey, a major of the National Guard. Moncey held out against the Russian troops, some of whom we see wounded in the foreground, until news of the Emperor's capitulation came through. The artist himself and his brother, Carle, were part of this brave but vain resistance, which marked the end of the reign of the Emperor, and the restoration of the monarchy under Louis XVIII.

Why the gates?

Since 1785 Paris had been surrounded by the Wall of the Farmers General, with gateways - a series of Neoclassical monuments by the architect Ledoux - which served as customs posts. The gates, like the Bastille, were seen as symbols of royal injustice, and on 13 July 1789 the Parisians took them by storm. All that remains today are those of Nation and Denfert-Rochereau, together with the rotunda of La Villette and Monceau. On the site of the Clichy gateway is the Place de Clichy where a statue of Moncey now stands.

▶▶ *To continue this tour, go back down to the first floor, then head to the Richelieu wing on the right (the journey is a long one, you are advised to use the floor plans at the back of this guide).*

The death of a palace

The construction of the Tuileries Palace, home to Catherine de Médicis, started in 1564. Extended and transformed, it became the main royal residence, but was eclipsed by Versailles in the late 18th century. Louis XVI lived there under house arrest in 1789, until his execution in 1792. The Convention turned it into its "National Palace", but in 1800 the First Consul Napoleon, who subsequently became Emperor, took up residence there, as did his successors, until Napoleon III.

The pomp of the imperial court

This throne was designed by the Emperor's architects, Percier and Fontaine. They are also responsible for the arch of the Carrousel, which marked the entrance to the court of the Tuileries Palace. It is a fine illustration of the Empire style, marked by references to Antiquity.

▸ François-Honoré-Georges Jacob-Desmalter, based on a design by Percier and Fontaine, *Napoleon I's throne at the Tuileries*, 1804. Gilded wood. 122 x 87 x 70 cm.

What are the symbols chosen for this piece of furniture?
The N of Napoleon is immediately visible, but also the imperial eagle borrowed from the Roman emblems, the sash of the Legion of Honour, and bees, symbols of work and fecundity, chosen by the Emperor to replace the fleur-de-lys.

In the family tradition

This is an "Imperial-style bed", a ceremonial canopy bed with a separating gilded rail. The king's bedroom in Versailles and the Tuileries was a highly symbolic place, where were held ceremonies for the king's morning rise and his return to bed in the presence of the court. The fleurs-de-lys are symbols of the Restoration monarchy.

◄ King's bedroom, bedroom furniture from the bedroom of Louis XVIII, then Charles X at the Tuileries.

Did the king really sleep in this bed?
No, it was simply a ceremonial bedroom. His real bedroom had a simpler decor, and was easier to heat in winter. The blue silk velvet hangings that accompanied the bed were produced in Lyon, in one of the finest factories of the time.

▶▶ *Go back and turn right into the service corridor (Room 82), from where you can access "Napoleon III's apartments". Notice the luxury of the dining room and the view on the Tuileries from the small rooms that precede the main salon.*

The apotheosis of the Imperial style

The Grand Salon is the crowning glory of the architectural and decorative fireworks that precede it. Even after the smaller salons and dining rooms that formed the apartment of the Duke of Morny, the minister of state and half-brother of Napoleon III, the sumptuous decor of this ceremonial salon is still amazing. By the Second Empire, Neoclassicism was outmoded, and the new fashion was "eclecticism". This architectural and decorative current drew from both medieval and Renaissance styles, but also from the grand classical French styles of the 17th and 18th centuries.

How come these apartments have been preserved?
Until 1993 they were occupied by the Finance Minister, before the ministry itself moved to Bercy, east Paris. One can understand that ministers were reluctant to leave such an environment! On the ceiling are four allegories representing the history of the Louvre: François I and the first project, Catherine de Médicis and the Tuileries, Henri IV and the Grand Gallery, Louis XIV and the colonnade.

▾ Grand Salon of the "Napoleon III apartments", 1859-61.

Lower ground floor

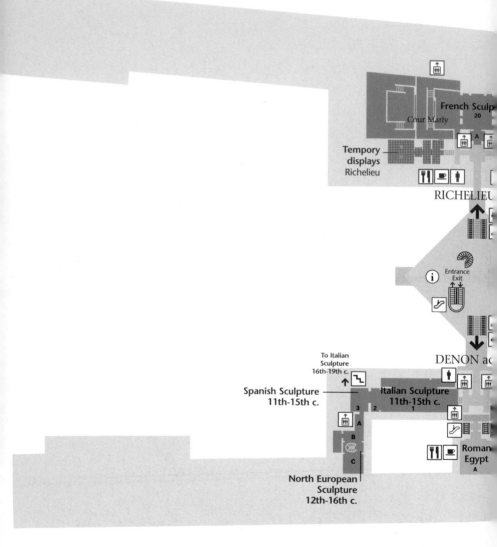

French Sculp 20

Cour Marly

Tempory
displays
Richelieu

RICHELIEU

Entrance
Exit

To Italian
Sculpture
16th-19th c.

Spanish Sculpture
11th-15th c.

Italian Sculpture
11th-15th c.

DENON a

Roman
Egypt

North European
Sculpture
12th-16th c.

The starting points of all nine guided tours are indicated
on the floorplans as well as the masterpieces of the masterpiece tour.

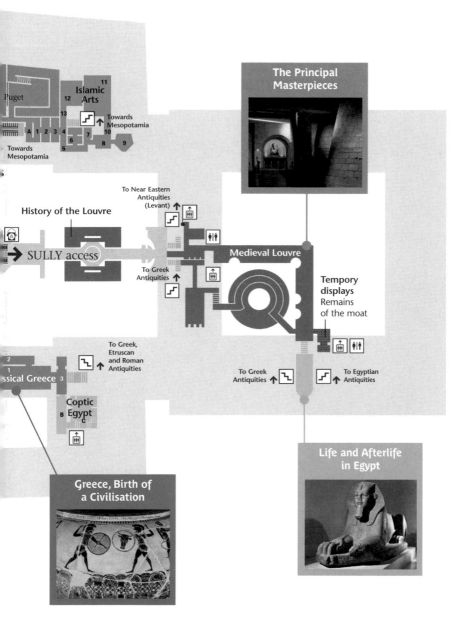

Puget

11

Islamic Arts

12

13

A 1 2 3 4

5 6 7 8 9

10

Towards Mesopotamia

Towards Mesopotamia

The Principal Masterpieces

To Near Eastern Antiquities (Levant)

History of the Louvre

SULLY access

To Greek Antiquities

Medieval Louvre

Tempory displays
Remains of the moat

To Greek, Etruscan and Roman Antiquities

2

1

ssical Greece 3

Coptic Egypt

B

C

To Greek Antiquities

To Egyptian Antiquities

Greece, Birth of a Civilisation

Life and Afterlife in Egypt

ground floor

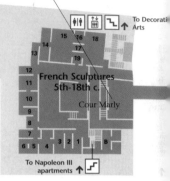

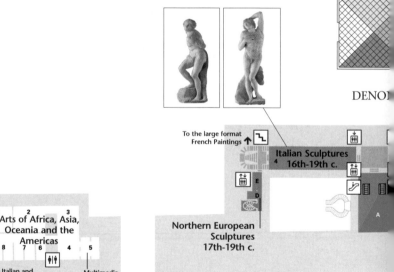

To Decorati
Arts

15 16 18
17
14
19
13

12
11   French Sculptures
10   5th-18th c.
9   Cour Marly
8
7
6 5   4   3 2 1   B

To Napoleon III
apartments

To the large format
French Paintings

Italian Sculptures
4   16th-19th c.

E

D

Northern European
Sculptures
17th-19th c.

A

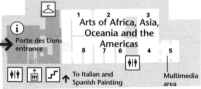

Porte des Lions
entrance

1   2   3
Arts of Africa, Asia,
Oceania and the
Americas
8   7   6   4   5

To Italian and
Spanish Painting

Multimedia
area

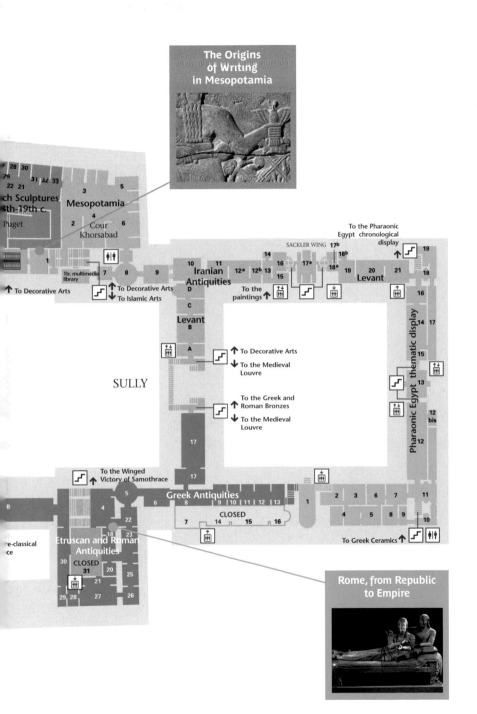

1st floor

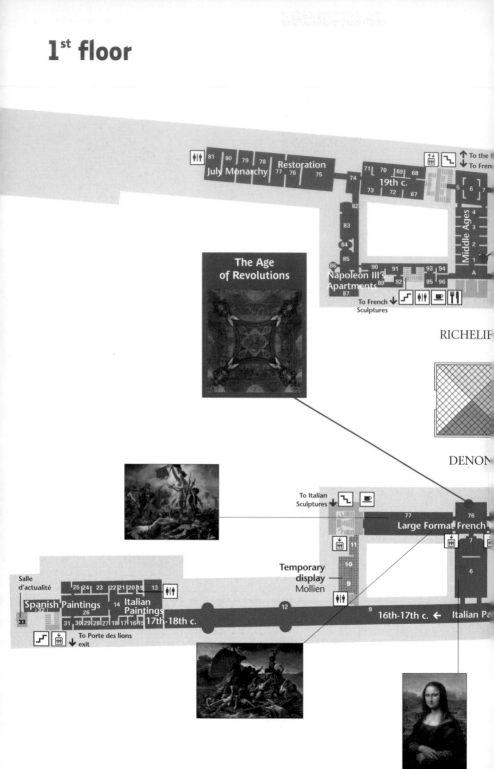

To the
To Fren

81 80 79 78 Restoration
July Monarchy 77 76 75

71 70 69 68
19th c.
73 72 67

74

82

83

84

85

86

90 91 93 94
Napoleon III's 89 92 95 96
Apartments 87

To French ↓
Sculptures

The Age
of Revolutions

Middle Ages
5 6 7
4
3
2
1
A

RICHELIF

DENON

To Italian
Sculptures ↓

77 76
Large Format French
11
7
Temporary 10
display 6
Mollien 8

Salle
d'actualité
25 24 23 22 21 20 19 13
Spanish Paintings 14 Italian
32 Paintings
33 26 17th-18th c.
31 30 29 28 27 18 17 16 15

16th-17th c. ← Italian Pa

12

To Porte des lions ↓
exit

138

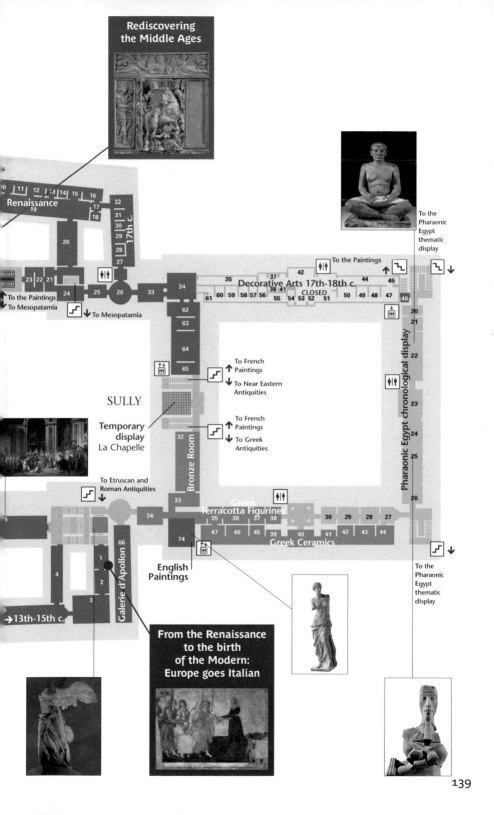

Rediscovering the Middle Ages

Renaissance

0 11 12 13 14 15 16
19
17
18

17th c.

32
31
30
29
28
27

20

23 22 21
24 25 26 33 34

To the Paintings
To Mesopatamia
To Mesopatamia

To the Paintings

35 37 42 44 45
Decorative Arts 17th-18th c.
38 41
61 60 59 58 57 56 55 54 53 52 51 50 49 48 47 46
CLOSED

To the Pharaonic Egypt thematic display

Pharaonic Egypt chronological display

20
21
22

62
63

64
65

To French Paintings
To Near Eastern Antiquities

23

SULLY

Temporary display
La Chapelle

To French Paintings
To Greek Antiquities

25

32

Bronze Room

To Etruscan and Roman Antiquities

26

33
34

Greek Terracotta Figurines
35 36 37 38
30 29 28 27

74

47 46 45 39 40 41 42 43 44
Greek Ceramics

To the Pharaonic Egypt thematic display

English Paintings

66
1
2
3

Galerie d'Apollon

4
5

13th-15th c.

From the Renaissance to the birth of the Modern: Europe goes Italian

2nd floor

18th-19th c.

C B A
D E F

29 27 27 25 23 22
28 26 24 21

Flanders 17th c.

30
31
32
33

34 35 36 37 38 39

Holland 17th c.

20

17
18

Flanders 17th c.

19

↓ To d

RICHELI

DENO

Credits

Musée du Louvre / Étienne Revault: cover (background photo); p. 4-5; p. 37; p. 45; p. 46; p. 62; p. 70 - **Musée du Louvre / Daniel Lebée / Carine Déambrosis:** p. 51; p. 53; p. 55 - **Musée du Louvre / Pierre Philibert:** p. 82; p. 83; p. 84; p. 85; p. 87; p. 122-123 - **Musée du Louvre / Angèle Dequier:** p. 68; p. 107; p. 109 - **Musée du Louvre / Christian Décamps:** p. 35; p. 36; p. 37 - **Musée du Louvre / Georges Poncet:** p. 34 - **RMN / Daniel Arnaudet / Gérard Blot / Christian Jean / Jean Schormans:** p. 24 - **RMN / Christian Larrieu:** p. 32; p. 59 - **RMN / Franck Raux:** p. 40; p. 41 - **RMN / René-Gabriel Ojéda:** p. 42; p. 57; p. 73; p. 113 - **RMN / Hervé Lewandowski:** p. 48-49; p. 50; p. 56; p. 58; p. 60; p. 61; p. 68; p. 69 - **RMN / Les frères Chuzeville:** p. 66-67; p. 74 - **RMN / Gérard Blot:** p. 76 - **RMN / DR:** p. 75 - **Erich Lessing:** p. 6; p. 7; p. 8; p. 9; p. 11; p. 12-13; p. 14; p. 15; p. 16; p. 17; p. 18; p. 19; p. 20-21; p. 22; p. 23; p. 25; p. 26; p. 27; p. 28-29; p. 30; p. 31; p. 33; p. 38; p. 39; p. 43; p. 44; p. 45; p. 46; p. 54-55; p. 62; p. 64-65; p. 70; p. 71; p. 72; p. 77; p. 78-79; p. 80; p. 81; p. 86; p. 88; p. 89; p. 90-91; p. 92; p. 93; p. 94; p. 95; p. 96; p. 97; p. 98; p. 99; p. 100; p. 101; p. 102; p. 103; p. 104-105; p. 106-107; p. 108; p. 109; p. 110; p. 111; p. 112; p. 114; p. 115; p. 116; p. 117; p. 118; p. 119; p. 120; p. 121; p. 124; p. 125; p. 126; p. 127; p. 128; p. 129; p. 130; p. 131; p. 132; p. 133 - **B. Pell / Musée du Louvre: Graphics of floor plans - Maud Riemann:** illustrations of cuneiform signs, p. 23 - **Jean-Baptiste Berthelom:** illustrations of hieroglyphics, p.35.

First printed May 2008 by Pollina printers in Luçon, France, for Editions ACTES SUD, Le Méjan, Place Nina-Berberova, 13200 Arles, France.
Dépôt légal 1ʳᵉ édition: juin 2008 / N° impression: L47008 (Printed in France)